Koro Bessho

Identities
and Security
in East Asia

Routledge
Taylor & Francis Group

LONDON AND NEW YORK

Adelphi Paper **325**

First published March 1999 by **Oxford University Press** for
International Institute for Strategic Studies
23 Tavistock Street, London WC2E 7NQ

This reprint published by Routledge
2 Park Square, Milton Park, Abingdon, Oxon, OX14 4RN
For the International Institute for Strategic Studies
Arundel House, 13-15 Arundel Street, Temple Place, London, WC2R 3DX
www.iiss.org

Simultaneously published in the USA and Canada
By Routledge
711 Third Avenue, New York, NY 10017

Routledge is an imprint of the Taylor & Francis Group, an informa business

© International Institute for Strategic Studies 1999

Director John Chipman
Editor Gerald Segal
Assistant Editor Matthew Foley
Design and Production Mark Taylor

British Library Cataloguing in Publication Data
Data available

Library of Congress Cataloguing in Publication Data

ISBN 0-19-922421–8
ISSN 0567-932x

contents

maps & tables

glossary

AFTA	ASEAN Free Trade Area
APEC	Asia-Pacific Economic Cooperation forum
ARF	ASEAN Regional Forum
ASEAN	Association of South-East Asian Nations
ASEM	Asia–Europe Meeting
CCP	Chinese Communist Party
CEA	Chinese Economic Area
CEPT	Common Effective Preferential Tariff zone
CER	Closer Economic Relations agreement (Australia and New Zealand)
CGI	Consultative Group for Indonesia
CSCE	Conference on Security and Cooperation in Europe
EAEC	East Asia Economic Caucus
EAEG	East Asia Economic Group
EC	European Community
EEC	European Economic Community
EU	European Union
G-7	Group of Seven industrial countries
G-8	Group of Eight industrial countries
GATT	General Agreement on Tariffs and Trade
IAP	Individual Action Plan (APEC)
IGGI	Inter-Governmental Group on Indonesia

IRBM .... intermediate-range ballistic missile
JSDP .... Social Democratic Party of Japan
LDP .... Liberal Democratic Party (Japan)
NAFTA .... North American Free Trade Agreement
NIE .... Newly Industrialised Economy
NLD .... National League for Democracy (Myanmar)
ODA .... Overseas Development Assistance (Japan)
OECD .... Organisation for Economic Cooperation and Development
PECC .... Pacific Economic Cooperation Council
PMC .... Post-Ministerial Conference (ASEAN)
PRC .... People's Republic of China
SDF .... Self-Defense Force (Japan)
TAC .... Treaty of Amity and Cooperation (ASEAN)
WTO .... World Trade Organisation
ZOPFAN .... Zone of Peace, Freedom and Neutrality (ASEAN)

introduction

While East Asia has its share of flash-points, from the Korean Peninsula to the South China Sea, the region has been relatively free from large-scale combat in the 1990s. Under these circumstances, two opposing views of the future of East Asian security relations have emerged. Optimists argue that increased interdependence and the development of international fora will lead to a sense of community in the region, which will in turn facilitate cooperative security relations. Advocates of this view cite developments in the Asia-Pacific Economic Cooperation (APEC) forum and the Association of South-East Asian Nations (ASEAN) Regional Forum (ARF) as sure signs that East Asia is moving towards this benign future.[1] Others, however, forecast more volatile conditions characterised by balance-of-power politics reminiscent of nineteenth-century Europe. Proponents of this view predict either the re-emergence of old conflicts that lay dormant during the Cold War, or the onset of new problems such as energy and food scarcity. Without the institutional frameworks to deal effectively with these difficulties, competition between nations will increase.[2]

Whichever view prevails, China and Japan, given their size, power and status in the international community, are likely to bear much of the responsibility for maintaining East Asia's stability. However, both countries have been reluctant to adopt a leadership role, while China has itself often been seen as a source of instability. By contrast, South-east Asia, through ASEAN, has been willing to take the initiative outside of its sub-region, and has shown how

Map 1 *East Asia*

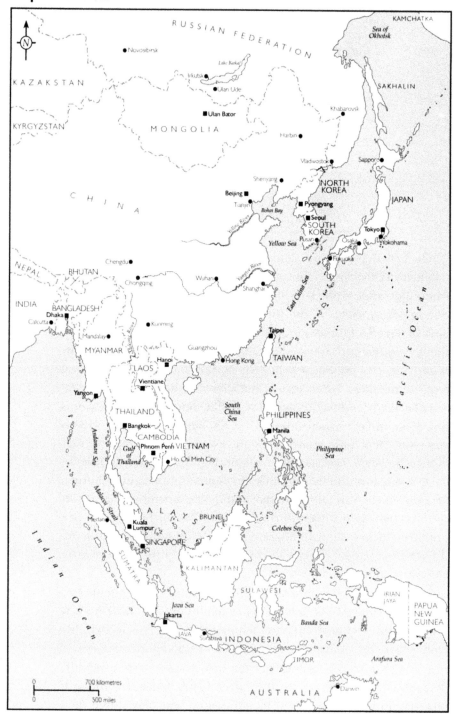

unity can be forged from diversity. However, South-east Asia does not have the resources or the authority to lead the whole of East Asia, especially after the financial crisis of 1997–98.

The states of East Asia seem still to be in the process of adjusting to the greater unpredictability of post-Cold War international relations. In this new environment, issues of identity can be as crucial as questions of national interest. The influences shaping a nation's sense of itself include not only relatively static elements like religion and ethnicity, but also more malleable factors such as national pride and past history. These ingredients can change in response to changing circumstances, notably alterations in relations with other states. This paper analyses the way in which these senses of identity have affected the actions of the key players in East Asia, and assesses future challenges and possibilities in the search for regional security.

chapter 1

Japan: Reluctant Leader?

Japan is often seen as caught between two conflicting identities: Asian and Western. The country seems to have succeeded in becoming a modern, industrialised nation without losing its distinct heritage or personality. At the same time, its sense of self seems torn between Asia and the West. In the more practical world of politics and security, both Japanese and non-Japanese alike have complained that the country has neither assumed the leadership role in Asia that it should, nor been a prominent advocate of Asian points of view on the world stage: an economic giant, but a political lightweight. Conversely, concern over the ramifications of a greater Japanese involvement in security affairs persists, both at home and abroad. For Yoshibumi Wakamiya, 'Japan's political outlook on Asia is a mixture of feelings of superiority and indebtedness, and of affinity and alienation'.[1]

This ambivalence in the way in which Japan sees itself, and is seen by its neighbours, stems not from any 'cultural' or 'civilisational' characteristics, but from the history of the country's dealings with Asians and Westerners. Japan's identity has been profoundly shaped by the international environment, and has undergone important changes at turning-points in the country's history such as the Meiji Restoration of 1868 and defeat in the Second World War. The rise of East Asia's economies and the end of the Cold War, together with the prolonged stagnation of the Japanese economy, have significantly affected Japan's identity, and may in turn alter the country's relations, both with Asia and with the wider world.

Japan's Dilemma

Since the mid-nineteenth century, two competing schools of thought have dominated Japanese views of the outside world: the 'Asianist', and the 'Euro-Americanist'. After the Meiji Restoration, which abolished Japan's traditional feudal structure, the belief that the country should 'leave Asia to enter Europe' became predominant within the political élite.[2] The *samurai* (warriors) who brought down the isolationist regime of the Tokugawa *shogunate* (military government) did so under the slogan *son-no jo-i* ('worship the emperor, and fight off foreigners'). However, the Restoration leaders quickly concluded that to resist US and European pressure was futile, abandoned their stated isolationism and instead decided to learn from the West. Under the banner *wakon yosai* ('Japanese spirit, Western technology'), the country absorbed European technology and, to an extent, adopted its lifestyle and political system. These changes were essentially pragmatic, far-reaching in form rather than in spirit: the aim was to build 'a rich nation and a strong army' (*fukoku kyohei*) to gain the West's respect.

'Japanese spirit, Western technology'

By contrast, Asianism in Japan up to the mid-twentieth century was more an idealistic than pragmatic response to Western encroachment. When Sun Yat-sen, the leader of the Chinese revolution of 1911, addressed a Japanese audience in 1924, his appeal for a 'great Asia', through which the region could achieve equality with the West and liberation from colonialism, met with a receptive response, although it was not clear how these aims might be achieved. Asianism became the ideological justification for Japan's claim to dominance in East Asia. The idea of a united 'Asia for Asians' was used to legitimise Japanese imperialism to secure and monopolise Asia's resources and markets under the Greater East Asia Co-Prosperity Sphere, first announced in 1938. Japan had 'left' Asia only to 'return' in the guise of the Western colonial states that it tried to supplant. Although Japan's post-war identity problems are of a different nature, the bitter experiences of Japanese militarism before 1945 continue to shape the country's outlook, both to the rest of Asia and to the world at large.

The Second World War destroyed Japan's military machine and its economy, and rid the country of its ambitions to dominate

Asia; after the conflict, its isolation was complete. The country's immediate task was to re-establish its sense of orientation, rebuild its economy and find its way back into the international community. The Constitutional Law introduced by the Allied occupation author-ities in November 1946 embodied principles of liberal democracy, pacifism and egalitarianism. Although for the Allies the Constitution was designed primarily to prevent Japan from again posing a military threat, its provisions were welcomed by the Japanese public as a fresh start after the country's experience of totalitarian mili-tarism. Unlike Japan's earlier encounter with Western ideas under the Meiji Restoration, after the Second World War these values were accepted in themselves, rather than as a means to a pragmatic end. As a result, Japan identified itself as one of the industrialised democracies of the West, and reconciled itself with the US. Washington helped Japan to re-enter the international community, with membership of the General Agreement on Tariffs and Trade (GATT) in 1955, of the UN in 1956 and of the Organisation for Economic Cooperation and Development (OECD) in 1964.

Despite the consensus in favour of the values embodied in the country's post-war Constitution, some, notably pacifism, caused problems. While the concept itself, as the opposite of the country's catastrophic militarism, won widespread support, there was dis-agreement over what it meant in practice. The question of how to promote the values of liberal democracy in East Asia, particularly human rights, also posed problems. These dilemmas often led Japan to eschew a leadership role in the region.

Pacificism

Under Article 9 of the Japanese Constitution, the 'Japanese people forever renounce war ... and the threat or use of force as a means of settling international disputes ... in order to accomplish this aim ... land, sea, and air forces, as well as other war potential, will never be maintained'.[3] This unprecedented article has caused debate since it came into effect in 1947. The interpretation developed by Japan's post-war governments forbids the country from sending troops overseas for the purpose of using force, but allows it to maintain a military for self-defence. As the Cold War deepened, the US reversed its policy towards Japan's military capability and urged Tokyo to revise its 'Peace Constitution' and remilitarise. Under Prime

Minister Shigeru Yoshida, Japan refused, although it did accede to US pressure to sign Second World War peace treaties only with states allied to Washington. In return, the US–Japan Security Treaty, initially agreed in 1951, ensured US protection.

Article 9's interpretation was long protested by the country's main post-war opposition party, the Social Democratic Party of Japan (JSDP), which argued that self-defence forces and participation in peacekeeping operations were unconstitutional, and that the US–Japan Security Treaty should be abolished. (The JSDP reversed its position when it came to power in 1994.) The JSDP was in effect advocating neutrality without armament – a type of isolationism sometimes referred to as 'one-country pacifism'. Any mention of using Japan's Self-Defense Force (SDF) outside the country, or of Japan intervening in international conflicts, prompted strong opposition, both from the JSDP and from 'progressive' intellectuals.

These two incompatible views divided the country, allowing no common ground for a meaningful debate on national security. The taboo on discussing military issues was broken only in the early 1980s, when Yasuhiro Nakasone became Prime Minister and initiated a debate on these matters.[4] In 1990, during the Gulf crisis, Japan's policy of not exporting weapons led to debate over whether it was acceptable to send gas-masks to Japanese Embassy staff in the region. No serious public discussion of how the SDF should cooperate with US forces in the event of a crisis took place until the 'Japan–US Joint Declaration on Security', which was issued during President Bill Clinton's visit to Japan in April 1996.

Internationally, the turning-point in Japan's role came when the country joined the West in imposing sanctions against the Soviet Union in response to its invasion of Afghanistan in 1979. Although primarily economic, Japan's involvement also meant participation in a joint political action, thus marking a break with post-war practice. The build-up of Soviet forces in the Far East and the deployment of SS20 intermediate-range ballistic missiles (IRBMs) in the early 1980s compelled Japan to stress the need for the Western bloc to act together to deal with the Soviet Union in Asia. Specifically, Japan

a turning-point in Japan's role

cautioned that Western Europe could not be content with securing the removal of SS20s from Europe if Moscow simply transferred them to Asia. These concerns led the Group of Seven (G-7) industrial nations to declare the indivisibility of Western security in a Political Statement issued at the Williamsburg Summit in 1983.[5] Japan's insistence on being included in debates over Western security was seen at the time as a bold step forward by both the political left and the right in Japan.

Nonetheless, Japan's reluctance to become involved in matters requiring discussion of military-related affairs persisted. Despite its strong economic position in South-east Asia, the country played a relatively limited role during the Cambodian war of the 1980s. Apart from putting forward general ideas, Tokyo for the most part simply stated its support for ASEAN, and pledged that it would contribute to Indochina's reconstruction once the conflict was resolved. This approach may have been partly the result of Tokyo's desire not to upset the ASEAN states. During a visit to ASEAN members in 1974, Prime Minister Kakuei Tanaka was greeted by violent protests against Japan's perceived economic 'invasion' of the region. But Tokyo's reluctance to become too deeply involved in an issue with military implications also shaped its approach. Only in the 1990s did Japan begin to send peacekeeping personnel to Cambodia.

Liberal Democracy and Human Rights

Liberal concepts such as freedom, democracy and human rights were not controversial in post-war Japan, but the country generally lacked the missionary zeal of Americans or Europeans in propagating these ideas overseas. Until South Korea's democratisation began in the late 1980s, Japan had no close neighbour sharing the same key values. Pushing for human rights overseas could therefore have risked further alienation in East Asia. Successive governments were also wary of charges of hypocrisy stemming from the country's colonial conduct. Finally, there was concern that direct coercion, sanctions for example, might make targeted countries more, rather than less, intransigent over human-rights issues. Japan stressed this view to its G-7 partners following the Tiananmen Square incident in China in 1989. Although Tokyo did not oppose economic measures against China, it argued at the G-7 Summit in Houston in 1990 that

Beijing should be encouraged to continue reform, and stated that Japan would eventually resume soft loans. With East Asian states becoming more vocal in expressing their own views on human rights, and economic sanctions in many cases not having the desired result, this issue has remained a difficult one for Japan.

Relations with East Asia

Japan's identification of itself with the Western bloc, both politically and in terms of its values, generally meant that it viewed its relations with East Asia in the context of US strategic priorities. According to Kazuo Ogura:

> *Japan's Asia policy is based on cold calculation and a strategy that takes into consideration the overall international situation and global order ... The Asia strategy that the United States (and, in turn, Japan) has followed – economic prosperity and democratisation in Asia and maintenance of American influence in the region – is gradually bearing fruit ... And by helping to implement this strategy, Japan is sharing in Asia's peace and prosperity.*[6]

Although this perceived 'subordination' to Washington prompted continued criticism, particularly from liberals and the left, the general perception of Japan as *in* Asia, but not necessarily *of* Asia, meant that the country's relationship with the US enjoyed basic support.

Despite this confidence in the merits of alliance with the US and of Japan's broader identification with the West, there was a widely shared feeling that the Japanese should be more under-standing of, and sympathetic to, East Asia than either Europeans or Americans. In a revision to the late-nineteenth century view that Japan should be a link between Asia and the West, many in post-war Japan felt that the country should 'build a bridge' from the West to Asia. Within the industrialised West, Japan claimed that it best understood Asia and Asian ways, and that it represented the region's interests. Before each annual G-7 summit, Japan sent envoys to its neighbours to gather their views and wishes; after each meeting, it sent rep-

Japan in *Asia, but not* of *Asia*

resentatives to brief them on the discussions that had taken place. This practice strengthened cooperative relations between Japan and its neighbours, while at the same time adding weight to its views in the G-7.

A Maturing Identity?

The 1990s have seen the end of the Cold War, the Gulf conflict of 1990–91 and the fiftieth anniversary of the end of the Second World War. While the basic framework of Japan's approach to the outside world has not changed, these developments appear to have made the country's key dilemmas less acute, and allowed it to adopt a less ambivalent position. The Japan–US security relationship, the cornerstone of Japan's foreign policy since the Second World War, lost its original *raison d'être* with the Soviet Union's demise. However, developments in Japan's security thinking triggered by instability on the Korean Peninsula, together with reduced economic tensions with the US in the mid-1980s, have allowed Washington and Tokyo to reaffirm the importance of their relationship. The Cold War's end also affected Japan's relations with the rest of East Asia by requiring the country to clarify its position regarding liberal values such as human rights, and also its stance towards its own past. Japan's efforts to meet these challenges, while neither fully satisfying its neighbours nor resolving its identity dilemmas, may nonetheless help the country to develop a more confident foreign-policy style.

Reconfirming the Japan–US Alliance

The end of the Cold War brought controversial US–Japan issues such as trade to the fore, and raised fundamental questions about the continued utility of the security alliance between the two countries. Japanese confidence, bordering on arrogance, in the country's economic strength and management style aggravated US frustration with the bilateral trade imbalance, leading to calls for greater unilateralism and trade sanctions. Literature in both Japan and the US fed resentment on both sides. Some US commentators argued that, with the end of communism, Japan had become America's major adversary; some in Japan held that it was time to 'leave America to enter Asia'. In a related, albeit uncontroversial, move, the Japanese Foreign Ministry was reorganised in August 1993, when the Foreign Policy Bureau was created as a coordinating body. The stated purpose of the reform was to respond to domestic criticism of the poor coordination between Foreign Ministry bureaux that had made it difficult for the ministry to respond effectively to the Gulf crisis. However, the Japanese media and outside observers saw the move as reflecting the post-Cold War decline in the importance of the North American Bureau.[7]

By the mid-1990s, relations between Japan and the US had improved. The conclusion of GATT's Uruguay Round and the establishment of the World Trade Organisation (WTO) in January 1995 gave both countries a stronger dispute-settlement mechanism. The trade imbalance declined, while the bursting of Japan's 'bubble economy' combined with vigorous growth in the US to transform American perceptions. Far from being a larger-than-life threat, Japan now seemed an ailing and ageing society facing major problems.

More fundamental to the reaffirmation of the Japan–US alliance was the realisation on both sides that the continued presence of the US in East Asia, for which the alliance provided the basis, was critical to the region's stability and prosperity. During a visit to Singapore in January 1997, Prime Minister Ryutaro Hashimoto made an important speech in which he argued that 'the presence of the United States, a country of unrivalled power and founded upon principles such as democracy, [the] market mechanism, and respect for creativity, is essential'; the Japan–US security treaty was 'a sort of infrastructure for stability and economic prosperity in the Asia Pacific ... Japan will continue to do its utmost to maintain confidence in the arrangements'.[8] Japan's decision to maintain its US link was taken not simply out of habit, nor was it based purely on US strategic aims. Rather, Japan had reconsidered its own security and the stability of East Asia as a whole after the Cold War, and had concluded that the alliance remained vital. The importance of the Japan–US alliance notwithstanding, the relationship has not been trouble-free. The issue of US bases on Okinawa, triggered by the rape of a schoolgirl by US servicemen in 1995, persists, while trade problems can occasionally flare up. But the relationship has survived its immediate post-Cold War test.

New Foreign-Policy Guidelines

Japan's pacifism and liberal democracy, combined with its reluctance to be seen as 'dominating' or 'leading' East Asia, meant that during

the Cold War it did not play an international political role com-
mensurate with its economic weight. In this it was assisted by the
Cold War's bipolarity, which tended to subordinate individual
countries' actions to the needs of alliance. By the early 1990s,
however:

> *one of the responsibilities of Japan, which has become capable
> of influencing the construction of an international order, is to
> articulate the philosophy of [its] foreign policy and to make
> clear constantly to the international community the ideals
> and objectives which Japan pursues internationally.*[9]

In an effort to achieve this clarity, the country took three specific
measures. First, it formulated new guidelines governing the pro-
vision of overseas aid. Under the Overseas Development Assistance
(ODA) Charter, announced in June 1992, aid became dependent on a
variety of factors, including a potential recipient's environmental
record, levels of military expenditure and arms exports and stance
on the non-proliferation of weapons of mass destruction (WMD).
Positions on democracy and human rights were also to be taken into
account.[10] The Charter signalled Japan's new-found willingness to
use aid to promote its preferred values and ideas, although the
country has been cautious in applying specific measures.

Secondly, Japan altered the guidelines governing its military
posture in the light of the 1990–91 Gulf crisis and North Korea's
suspected nuclear-weapons' programme, which made clear the
extent to which Japan was unprepared for security developments in
the Asia-Pacific. Throughout the Gulf crisis, the Japanese public was
adamantly against sending SDF forces abroad for combat. At the
same time, however, it seemed that
the country would be more willing to *Japan modernises*
support a contribution to internat- *its foreign policy*
ional peace and stability that went
beyond the merely financial. Since the Gulf conflict, SDF personnel
have participated in mine-sweeping operations in the Gulf, and have
been deployed as peacekeepers in Angola, Cambodia, El Salvador
and Mozambique, and as part of the UN Disengagement Observer
Force (UNDOF) on the Golan Heights. They have also taken part in
humanitarian missions for Rwandan refugees in Zaire (now the

Table I *Top Ten Recipients of Japanese Overseas Development Assistance, 1997*

(US$m net)

China	576.86
Indonesia	496.86
India	491.80
Thailand	468.26
Philippines	318.98
Vietnam	232.48
Jordan	139.63
Sri Lanka	134.56
Bangladesh	129.98
Egypt	125.40
Sub-total	3,114.82
Total ODA	6,612.59

Source   *Japan's Official Development Assistance Annual Report, 1998* (Tokyo: Ministry of Foreign Affairs, 1998), p. 119

Democratic Republic of Congo). In November 1995, Japan's National Defense Programme Outline was revised for the first time in 19 years. Under the new Outline, 'defense capability is to be expanded to encompass not only national defense … but also response to large-scale disasters … as well as contribute to the creation of a more stable security environment'.[11] The 'Japan–US Joint Declaration on Security' announced in April 1996 initiated a review of the Japan–US Defence Cooperation Guidelines established in 1978, the results of which were announced in September 1997. The new Guidelines stipulated the nature of US–Japanese cooperation 'under normal circumstances'; in 'actions in response to an armed attack against Japan'; and in 'cooperation in situations in areas surrounding Japan that will have an important influence on Japan's peace and security'.[12] The Annex to the Guidelines identified several fields of permissible SDF activity outside Japan, including relief operations and dealing with refugees; search and rescue; and non-combatant evacuation. The review met with a mixed response from Japan's neighbours. Most neighbouring governments cautiously welcomed it, with the proviso that they wanted continued transparency, while China remained sceptical at best. In making clear to its neighbours what its armed forces would do in a crisis, Japan sought to provide the clarity that it felt would ease fears of its possible rise to military power. One major purpose of issuing the new Guidelines was therefore to provide the transparency that Japan's neighbours, as well as its own people, sought.[13]

Japan's possible candidacy for Permanent Membership of the UN Security Council has played an important role in the pacifism debate. Some in Japan, Shusei Tanaka, Special Assistant to Prime Minister Morihiro Hosokawa, for example, argued against membership on the grounds that it would entail military activity on a par with that undertaken by the existing Permanent Members.[14] In his statement at the fiftieth session of the UN General Assembly in September 1995, Foreign Minister Yohei Kono declared Japan ready to discharge the responsibilities of Permanent Membership of the Security Council. At the same time, however, Kono made clear that this would not include modifying the provisions of Japan's 'Peace Constitution'. Debate between those keen to see Japan become a 'normal' country with a 'normal' role for its military, and those who argue that it should remain a 'civilian power', persists.[15] Conservatives in the US may still complain that Japan is not doing enough in security affairs. However, the nervous response of Japan's neighbours to the new Guidelines for security cooperation suggests that both Tokyo and Washington should remain cautious in their approach to military issues.

The third step that Japan took in reshaping its foreign policy was to address its pre-1945 record. On 15 August 1995, the fiftieth anniversary of the end of the Second World War, Prime Minister Tomiichi Murayama issued a statement acknowledging that Japan, 'through its colonial rule and aggression', caused 'tremendous damage and suffering to the people of many countries', and expressing 'feelings of deep remorse'.[16] Japanese leaders had made similar statements before. Murayama's apology was not, however, that of an individual politician, but had been officially approved by the

Cabinet, and signed by Murayama (a Social Democrat), the conservative Liberal Democratic Party (LDP) leader and Foreign Minister Kono and by Hashimoto, who succeeded Murayama as Prime Minister in January 1996. The Joint Declaration issued during South Korean President Kim Dae Jung's visit to Japan in 1998 expressed 'deep remorse and heartfelt apology' for the 'damage and suffering' Japan had caused the Korean people during 'a certain period in the past'.[17]

Future Challenges

During the 1990s, Japan increasingly felt that, through economic development and democratisation, notably in South Korea, its neighbours were moving closer to its values and principles. East Asian countries were no longer simply the objects of a policy implemented in coordination with the US, but had become 'dialogue partners' to whom Japan tried to explain its policy and the importance of its US alliance; to clarify its stance on key values like democracy, human rights and pacifism; and to more convincingly atone for its past. Japan has become far more active in these areas than before, but, by virtue of its history and affinity with its neighbours, has taken positions that differ from those of the other Western powers.

Japan's identity dilemma is becoming less acute, and the country may become better able to assume a leading role in shaping the international environment. This outcome is not, however, guaranteed. It presupposes that East Asia's progress towards broadly Western values is inevitable, but a vocal school of thought argues that, far from converging, the region should carve out a distinct 'Asian way'. If so, East Asia's economic development may not bring it as close to Japan as expected. Second, it is debatable whether Japan's easing identity dilemma will automatically lead the country to assume a greater leadership role in East Asia. Since the Second World War, Japan has sought to emulate the West, rather than setting its own standards or introducing new ideas. Japan's efforts to bridge the gap between the West and Asia have sometimes been criticised as taking the middle ground, rather than expressing a firm position of its own.[18] If the country is to take on a greater leadership role in East Asia, it needs original policies based on its long-term national interests.

East Asia's financial crisis of 1997–98 exacerbated some of the problems that had arisen earlier in the decade by denting Japan's self-confidence. In the short term, the country needs to recognise that whatever influence and respect it may enjoy has stemmed largely from its ability to lead the East Asian economies, and thus to contribute to regional stability. Allowing the region's economies to disintegrate will undermine decades of effort, both by Japan and by the US. Japan needs to reform its own economy and lead the way out of the gloom. In the longer term, with regained confidence the country will need to carry forward the development begun in the early 1990s to stimulate original thinking and a more active leadership role, both in its relations with its neighbours and with the wider world.

chapter 2

China: Future Leader?

Like Japan, China has shown little willingness to lead in East Asia. This reluctance is partly the result of domestic political and economic preoccupations, but, again like Japan, also stems from identity problems. China during the 1990s has presented two very different faces to the world. The Tiananmen Square incident in 1989, nuclear tests in 1995 and 1996, and tension in the Taiwan Straits have created an image of China as a resentful, disruptive nation willing, at times, to be at loggerheads with the international community. On the other hand, Beijing's diplomatic actions in 1997 and 1998 suggest that China is aspiring to be seen as a responsible world power working for stability.

Following China's smooth handling of two key events in 1997 – the reversion of Hong Kong and the leadership transition in the wake of paramount leader Deng Xiaoping's death – conventional wisdom has it that the country will, at least for some years yet, continue the reform and opening process begun by Deng. Hence, it will seek to maintain the stable international environment conducive to such internal change. As Singapore's Senior Minister, Lee Kuan Yew, put it in late 1997, the leadership of Deng's successor, President Jiang Zemin, 'will thrive best in an atmosphere of stability and growth'.[1] However, the country faces a series of challenges which could threaten the reform process, including tackling its ailing state-owned enterprises, reducing corruption and strengthening the rule of law, and coping with the repercussions of decentralisation and unrest among non-Han ethnic groups. China's future, and its relations with the outside world, will also be shaped by the more complex question of the country's dual identity.

Stability Above All?

Memories of Tiananmen, nuclear tests and tension in the Taiwan Straits have fostered the perception in the West that China is a disruptive nation outside the international community's mainstream. However, China's diplomacy in 1997 and 1998 suggests that the country is aspiring to be seen as a responsible power working for a stable international environment. Jiang's state visit to the US in October 1997 was an important early move for Chinese post-Deng diplomacy. Beijing's insistence that the trip be treated as a state visit by a world leader suggests that it was, at least in part, designed to consolidate Jiang's position within the Chinese Communist Party (CCP). At the same time, however, the trip can be seen as an attempt by Beijing to portray China as America's equal; the joint statement issued after the meeting, for example, declared that 'the two Presidents are determined to build towards a constructive strategic partnership'.[2] China appeared genuinely interested in improving relations with Washington: it declared its intention to increase efforts to reduce nuclear proliferation and pledged significant tariff reductions by 2005. The US reciprocated by lifting its ban on sales of nuclear items to China. Although Beijing made clear its views on human rights, several weeks after the trip China freed one of its better-known dissidents, Wei Jingsheng, possibly reflecting a wish to live up to its own self-image as 'firm on principle but pragmatic'. Clinton's return visit to China in June–July 1998 seems to have consolidated the progress made the previous year by formalising the emerging partnership between the two countries.

China also made progress with other powers. It reached a milestone in its relations with Russia in November 1997, when the two countries resolved their long-standing border dispute. The move was part of efforts to elevate their relationship from 'constructive cooperation' to 'strategic partnership'. While this change may be more symbolic than real, the use of the word 'strategic' is important given China's aspirations for a 'strategic partnership' with the US. China's relations with Japan were strained in 1995–96, partly because of the question of past experiences, and partly because of China's nuclear tests, which prompted Japan to suspend grant aid. However, the atmosphere improved with Prime Minister Hashi-moto's visit in September 1997, which was returned by Chinese Premier Li Peng two months later. In February 1998, Chinese Defence Minister Chi Haotian travelled to Japan, the first such visit for 14 years. During the trip, both countries agreed to increase exchanges between their armed forces, including reciprocal visits by their chiefs of staff and, possibly, by their navies. Together with Jiang's visit to

China tries hard to seem a good citizen

India in December 1996, the first ever by a Chinese head of state, these initiatives indicate the application with which China has sought to present itself as an important and responsible member of the world community, on a par with the major powers.

Beijing has also tried to play a responsible role in some of East Asia's potentially most destabilising issues. China has made constructive contributions to the Four Party Talks over the Korean Peninsula, pointing out that it is the only participant enjoying diplomatic relations with the other three (the US and the two Koreas). At a meeting with ASEAN leaders in December 1997, Jiang stated that China would 'never seek hegemony', but would 'forever be a good neighbour, a good partner and a good friend with ASEAN countries'. Less predictably, he was reported to have proposed that unresolved disputes with several ASEAN nations over the sovereignty of islands in the South China Sea be 'shelved temporarily' to prevent them from impeding the development of good relations.[3] At the news conference following the meeting, Chinese Foreign Minister Qian Qichen claimed that there was 'no tension in the South China Sea', and described the sovereignty disputes as a 'historic legacy'.[4] From late 1997, China also called upon Taiwan to resume cross-Straits talks, which it did in 1998.

Mutual Distrust
Despite these developments, Western analysts continue to voice concerns about China's possible future behaviour as its economy expands. Abundant Western literature in the 1990s has warned of a coming conflict between China and the US.[5] Even those who take a

more sanguine view still sound a note of caution. While arguing that China 'will neither have the will nor the capability to exercise hegemony over Asia in the decades to come', David Shambaugh also believes that the US and China will 'become competitive rivals and possibly strategic adversaries'.[6] The relevant question for Western experts, as it was in Cold War debates over the Soviet Union, remains whether China should be engaged, or contained.[7] However frequently Chinese leaders claim not to seek hegemony, Western experts continue to discuss the possibility, turning to past patterns to suggest future trends. While Alastair Johnston argues that 'China's decision-makers and strategists have displayed a consistently *real politik* world view since 1949', Tomoyuki Kojima contends that 'the average life cycle of a given national policy has been from five to ten years: the eighteen year duration of Deng's reform policies was a notable exception'; 'signs of fatigue are obvious', suggesting a policy change in the near future.[8] Analysts have also noted China's tendency to resort to coercion, rather than persevere with diplomacy, to achieve its aims.

From China's perspective, these Western views presuppose that the country is, if not an adversary, at least an outsider. 'Engagement' seems a Western ploy to become involved in the country's affairs in order to bring about the peaceful collapse of the regime from within. Deng ended open debate on this point in 1992, when he strongly reaffirmed his intention to open up to the West. Nonetheless, many in China undoubtedly believe that the country is not viewed with the respect and trust worthy of a 'strategic partner'. The revision of the guidelines for Japan–US security cooperation seems an aggressive act of containment, rather than an attempt to clarify and consolidate cooperation between Tokyo and Washington. However, Chinese policy-makers must understand that the West's mistrust stems not from a sinister hidden motive or from any cynicism inherent in Western culture, but from the confusing message China sends to the world. On the one hand, the country wishes to see itself as a world power, and to be treated as such; on the other, it believes itself to be a weak developing nation still seeking redress for past injustices. These contradictory views co-exist and, although both are in some ways justified, their combination confuses assessments both by outsiders, and by the Chinese themselves.

China's Dual Identity
A World Power

China has never officially taken the position that it is a superpower, or that it is destined to become one. On the contrary, it has consistently claimed to be a champion of developing countries. It was a co-sponsor of the Asian–African Conference at Bandung, Indonesia, in 1955, the first international meeting of what became the non-aligned states. Under its conception of the three-world theory, China stood, not with the First World, but with the Third World of developing nations. This position became difficult to sustain following China's strategic alliance with the US against the Soviet Union in the 1970s. The multipolar post-Cold War world sought by China seems to remain based on an 'inner core' of itself, the US and Russia, both of which it has identified as 'strategic partners'. Although its military capability and economic strength do not allow it a global reach similar to that of the US, China has acted politically as a world power.

Several factors inform China's self-image as a global power, including its size, huge population and significant resources. The country's long and illustrious imperial history is also important. To its contemporaries, the Middle Kingdom was not simply Asia's largest state, but was the world itself, ruled by an Emperor mandated by Heaven. In theory, there were no boundaries between the Empire and neighbouring nations, which were *China sees Asia as its periphery, not its home region* seen as little more than 'barbarian' lands owing differing levels of allegiance to the Emperor. Thus, China is not part of Asia; Asia is China's periphery. Given this history, the belief in modern China as a world power comes naturally, while partnership with other Asian states does not. China does not yet appear to have found a comfortable way of dealing with its regional neighbours.

A Developing Nation

The contrasting – and more formally expressed – identity is of China as a weak and victimised developing nation. The reversion of Hong Kong to Chinese rule in July 1997 was celebrated with gusto in China, where it was seen as a symbolic event 'washing away one hundred years of national shame'. Jiang began his political report to the fifteenth CCP National Congress in September 1997 with a reference to China's humiliation in 1900, when eight foreign powers occupied Beijing, and narrated the country's twentieth-century history in terms of an effort to win national liberation.[9] Since 1993, China's Constitution has declared becoming 'wealthy and strong' (*fu qiang*) a national goal, indicating the lingering perception of the country as poor, weak and backward.

The slogan 'wealthy and strong' is reminiscent of that used in nineteenth-century Japan. Although it would be far-fetched to suggest that China, seeking to counter perceived 'imperialist pressure', could follow Japan's pre-war course, its conjunction of economic strength and military power has given its neighbours and the West pause for thought. Although Beijing may be interested in the South-east Asian model of development, the country's goals go beyond those of the 'development dictatorships', and will not be met until China has a 'strong army'. According to its self-image, China may be acting as a weak and victimised nation trying to put things right; its neighbours, on the other hand, may see it as a great power preparing to be more assertive. China's challenge is to recognise this perception, and to convince its neighbours that it has no intention of bullying them, even after it becomes economically stronger.

This is easier said than done. For example, China sees the Taiwan issue as a domestic matter, and therefore feels justified in using or threatening force in a bid to resolve it. Many South-east Asians outwardly agree that Taiwan is a domestic issue, and therefore no concern of theirs. Nevertheless, Chinese shows of force, and declarations that using force is the ultimate solution to a problem, make its neighbours uneasy. Although developments such as Hong Kong's return may weaken China's self-identification as a victim, the conventional view in the West is that the CCP will continue to promote this image because it will increasingly have to rely on nationalism to maintain its legitimacy given the general collapse of communism elsewhere. The problem of China's dual identity is thus likely to persist.

Sino-Japanese Rivalry?

How do the implications of China's dual identity affect the most important bilateral relationship in East Asia: the one between itself and Japan? Analysts such as Denny Roy have argued that 'an economically powerful China may provoke a military build-up by Japan' leading to a new 'cold war'. A 'burgeoning China' therefore poses 'a long-term danger to Asia-Pacific security'.[10] According to Singaporean Senior Minister Lee, the region 'has never at the same time experienced both a strong China and a strong Japan. Some tensions may be inevitable'.[11]

The nature of the Sino-Japanese relationship is, however, more complex. While relations between the two countries since the end of the Second World War have not been trouble-free, they have also not primarily been adversarial. Despite China's strong verbal attacks on Japan in the 1960s over its past imperialism and militarism, both countries had unofficial channels of communication before relations were normalised in 1972. Soon afterwards, China became one of the top recipients of Japanese overseas assistance, and bilateral trade links grew significantly. Despite difficulties over their shared past, China's nuclear tests and disputes over the Senkaku (Diaoyu) Islands, Japan has tended to advise the international community against isolating Beijing.

Future relations between the two countries will depend on three main factors: national sentiment, which appears to have hardened on both sides in the 1990s; China's military build-up and reactions to it in Japan; and possible competition for leadership in East Asia. China's resentment of its past treatment by Japan, coupled with Tokyo's more assertive approach to democracy and human rights in the region in the 1990s, suggest a

Asia has never known both a strong China and a strong Japan

possible clash. Up until the 1980s, Japanese sentiment towards China had been marked by a mix of warmth and guilt. Immediately after the end of the Second World War, Nationalist leader Chiang Kai-shek allowed many Japanese to return home, while, as it normalised relations with Japan in the 1970s, the People's Republic declared that it would not seek war reparations. In response, Tokyo provided large amounts of official aid and other assistance. To many in Japan, China's post-war magnanimity suggested that, as it grew wealthier, the country would become a benevolent world power.

The suppression of students in Tiananmen Square in 1989 and China's nuclear tests in the mid-1990s fundamentally challenged this belief, and led Japan to suspend grant aid. The blasts – justified on the grounds that, compared with the other nuclear powers, China had conducted relatively few tests – touched a raw nerve in Japan, the only country ever to have suffered nuclear attack. Claims by Chinese officials that Japanese aid was in lieu of war reparations, and therefore that Tokyo had no right to suspend it, compounded the situation and undercut the goodwill that the earlier generation of Chinese leaders had cultivated. From China's point of view, continued insensitive remarks about the past by conservative Japanese politicians cancelled out expressions of remorse or apology made by the country's Prime Ministers. To coincide with the fiftieth anniversary of the end of the Second World War, Beijing launched a vigorous media campaign concerning Japan's actions during the conflict, thereby fuelling popular anti-Japanese feeling.

Although both China and Japan clearly need to make a determined effort to improve popular perceptions of each other, there are moderating forces on both sides. Fuelling nationalism may be useful to the CCP in its efforts to unite the nation and retain legitimacy, but the Party must be careful that it does not grow to the point where it comes to challenge the established order. When tensions rose over the sovereignty of the Senkaku (Diaoyu) Islands in 1996, prompting anti-Japanese demonstrations in Hong Kong and Taiwan, both Beijing and Tokyo were careful to prevent the situation from developing into a serious confrontation. In Japan, the 'romantic' view of a beneficent China may have faded, but policy-makers still appear overwhelmingly to believe that supporting Beijing's reform process is crucial if the country is to become a responsible world power.

China's military build-up is the second key issue affecting future Sino-Japanese relations. Chinese analysts are said to 'seem incredulous that Japan, given its history of aggression towards China dating back to the 1890s, could sincerely view China as a threat and alter its defense policy accordingly'.[12] This can be seen as a typical case of 'victimised-nation' thinking: turning a blind eye to the possibility that military expansion by a power of China's potential may be viewed with unease by its neighbours. It would, however, be wrong to assume that this military development will inevitably prompt an arms race between China and Japan. The presence of US forces in East Asia makes any over-reaction in

Table 2 *Chinese Military Expenditure, 1985–1998*

	GDP	Official Defence Budget	Estimated Real Military Expenditure
	(1997 US$bn)	(1997 US$m)	(1997 US$m)
1985	421	9,178	28,276
1986	423	8,008	21,879
1987	422	7,512	16,120
1988	456	7,519	16,211
1989	454	8,231	22,537
1990	452	7,101	25,166
1991	456	7,013	25,698
1992	512	7,564	27,030
1993	562	8,575	29,909
1994	578	6,788	30,412
1995	584	7,902	34,345
1996	629	8,768	36,176
1997	639	9,719	36,551
1998	689	10,775	36,268

Source IISS

response to Chinese modernisation unlikely. Even if the US presence declined, Japanese attitudes towards militarism would make domestic military expansion unacceptable. Japan did not greatly increase its military capability in the face of the Soviet build-up of forces in the Far East in the 1970s and 1980s, even though it was encouraged to do so by Beijing. In April 1980, Premier Hua Guofeng reportedly told Diet member Yasuhiro Nakasone that Japan should increase its defence spending; the Deputy Chief of General Staff of the People's Liberation Army (PLA) claimed that Japan need not keep to its self-imposed expenditure ceiling of 1% of gross national product (GNP).[13] However, the highest percentage reached in the following two decades was 1.013%, in 1988.

Finally, it appears unlikely that Japan and China will compete for leadership in East Asia in the foreseeable future since neither has shown itself willing to assume such a role. When they act as global players, they do so on different stages: China in the UN Security Council, and Japan in the G-8 forum. For China, its position as a Permanent Member sits well with its self-image as a world power; for Japan, G-8 status accords with its wish to be identified with the industrialised West. Both countries seem to insist on playing a lead role through these fora, but neither wants the burden of leadership, and neither is at present keen to usurp the other's place.

The question is not how to prevent rivalry developing over this issue, but how to bring the two countries together in a multilateral forum to work for East Asian stability. China may not welcome Japan's admission to Permanent Membership of the Security Council, while both countries have not worked as closely together as may have been hoped for in APEC or the ARF. China's response to a Japanese and US idea for a trilateral government-level meeting on security affairs, developed in 1997, has been that it 'has merit, but we should study this idea between academics for the time being'.[14] The first of such 'non-government' trilateral meetings took place in July 1998, with high-level participation from all three countries. This may lead to consultations at government level following agreement that officials could in the future participate in a personal capacity.[15]

A Hegemon To Be?

Western analysts continue to ask whether China will become a hegemonic power in the twenty-first century. This question may be necessary but, for the states of East Asia, it is insufficient. China's aspirations to fulfil its great potential cannot be denied. The question is thus what *kind* of world power it will become. Chinese leaders have repeatedly declared that they do not intend their country to be a 'hegemon' but, while these statements should not necessarily be met with scepticism, they do not fully answer the question.

The world, and East Asia in particular, needs China's active participation as a responsible power in specific security issues such as those pertaining to the Korean Peninsula, and in wider areas like energy and food security.[16] Following Asia's financial crisis in 1997–98, China was important to the recovery of the region's economies by not devaluating the *yuan* despite its lost competitiveness. China has thus come to be treated as a significant factor in financial affairs, as well as in trade issues. The prominent and favourable attention the country received in the wake of the crisis seems to have encouraged Chinese self-confidence and responsible behaviour. The challenge for the international community is to integrate this new economic power into the rule-based international system and, more

China has failed to reassure the world

specifically, into the WTO. This does not necessarily mean giving up preferential treatment as a developing nation: the benefits of further concessions from China must be weighed against the potential costs of China's perception of ill-treatment in this area, as long as the system's regulations and transparency are preserved.

After its show of force across the Taiwan Straits and its nuclear tests in 1995 and 1996, China seems to have changed its approach to that of a responsible power seeking stable relations in a multipolar world. Does this shift reflect a fundamental change in the way that China sees itself in the international community? Has the smooth handover of Hong Kong, for example, weakened China's self-image as a victimised nation, or is this new, moderate tone a tactical move designed to maintain stability while the country grows richer and stronger? China has failed to reassure the international community of its motives. The way in which it governs Hong Kong will be important in shaping international perceptions, but mutual distrust and the problem of China's dual identity will persist unless a stable and durable situation is established *vis-à-vis* Taiwan. In the meantime, Beijing can demonstrate its willingness to take a leading role without bullying its neighbours, by playing an active part as an equal partner in multilateral institutions. The international community should encourage and assist China to do so.

chapter 3

The 'ASEAN Way'?

Unlike China and Japan, the countries of South-east Asia have actively built structures in order to shape relations in their region. Their main tool for doing so has been ASEAN, which has made some progress in forging a common identity between its diverse members. The Association has played a significant international role through its Post-Ministerial Conferences (PMCs) with so-called 'dialogue partners', the ASEAN Regional Forum (ARF), and in groupings such as APEC and the Asia–Europe Meeting (ASEM).[1] Although ASEAN has neither achieved European Union-style integration nor actively sought to resolve disputes between its members, stability has been maintained, contributing to the region's economic development. ASEAN's success in creating unity from diversity has led some to propose the 'ASEAN way' as a model for North-east Asia, or for East Asia as a whole.[2]

Creating a Community

ASEAN was established on 8 August 1967 with the Bangkok Declaration, signed by Indonesia, Malaysia, the Philippines, Singapore and Thailand. Brunei joined the Association in 1984; Vietnam followed in 1995, and Laos and Myanmar in 1997. While there is basic agreement that Cambodia will be admitted, the country's domestic political problems have made the Association wary of specifying precisely when it will join. Both within and between themselves, ASEAN's member-states are diverse. Indonesia's

Map 2 *The ASEAN States*

Muslim population is the largest in the world; Thailand is devoutly Buddhist, the Philippines predominantly Catholic and Vietnam ruled by an officially atheist Communist Party. In 1996, Indonesia's GNP was $216 billion, that of Laos $1.9bn. Over ten million people live in Jakarta, three times the population of Singapore. Ethnically, ASEAN's members are equally varied.

At its founding, ASEAN was even more heterogeneous. Since its members were primarily agricultural economies, there was little economic interaction between them, while Indonesia, Malaysia and the Philippines retained close links with their former colonial powers. What the five original members shared, however, was the need to consolidate their authority as states, a project given added urgency by the experiences of divided Indochina. The Bangkok Declaration affirmed the five states' determination to 'ensure their stability and security from external interference' and to 'preserve their national identities', and set out ASEAN's three key aims:

- to 'accelerate economic growth, social progress and cultural development in the region';
- to 'promote regional peace and stability'; and
- to 'promote active collaboration and mutual assistance on matters of common interest'.[3]

ASEAN's principle of non-interference in the internal affairs of its members was crucial to maintaining its cohesion. A web of consultative meetings was established, and decisions taken only through consensus. This called for self-restraint from Indonesia, which accounted for over half of the total population of the Association's five founder-states. ASEAN's stance towards the domestic affairs of its members sat well with Indonesia's

ASEAN's purpose is to strengthen state sovereignty

guiding principles of *bhinneka tunggal ika* ('unity in diversity') and *musyawarah mufakat* ('careful discussion and consensus'). Similarly, the Association did not seek to resolve the many problems between its members. ASEAN's sense of solidarity has been more effective in creating the conditions for compromise, rather than acting in an official arbitration capacity.[4] The Treaty of Amity and Cooperation (TAC), signed in February 1976 by Indonesia, Malaysia, the Philippines, Singapore and Thailand, established a dispute-settlement mechanism, the High Council, but this has never been used.[5] Economically too the Association did not pursue official integration. Ad hoc ideas such as developing an 'ASEAN car', for example, have not been successful.

Aware of its weakness and of the need to avoid provoking external forces, ASEAN maintained a low profile in its external relations. Although the Bangkok Declaration stated as one of its aims the promoting of regional peace and stability, ASEAN did not assume a specifically security-related role and clearly rejected becoming a military alliance. The Association's security-related initiatives, such as establishing a Zone of Peace, Freedom and Neutrality (ZOPFAN) in 1971 and the Declaration of ASEAN Concord in 1976, were of more symbolic than real importance. Nonetheless, the anti-communism of its members prompted hostility from the Soviet Union, China and Vietnam, all of whom saw ASEAN as primarily a US-backed military grouping.

Although ASEAN was essentially designed to preserve its member-states' freedom from outside intervention, ASEAN states did accept outside help on a bilateral basis. While eschewing collective security, most members had security ties with the US or other outside powers. Member-states also accepted substantial economic aid from Japan. At the same time, while relying on the West as a bulwark against communism, the Association was wary of Western dominance in the region, and so sought to balance outside powers – namely Japan and the US – against each other.

This balancing act became the core of ASEAN's external policy. Whether prompted by the realisation that, even acting together, member-states could not counter one of the major powers, by Indonesia's position as leader of the Non-Aligned Movement, or by the simple failure to agree on a more active stance, ASEAN maintained an officially neutral status. To an extent, this position achieved the desired result. In the late 1970s, China dropped its antagonism towards ASEAN to give its full backing to the Association: 'China considered the activities of ASEAN "a blow to the ambitions of the superpowers, Soviet social imperialism in particular, to dominate South-East Asia"'.[6]

ASEAN faced its first real crisis in 1979, when Vietnam invaded Cambodia (then Kampuchea), toppling the Khmer Rouge regime and bringing Vietnamese forces to Thailand's border. Although ASEAN's members did not share a common view of the conflict – Thailand would have been a natural rival with Vietnam for influence in Indochina, while Indonesia and Malaysia would have seen Vietnam as a potential ally to counter Chinese influence – the challenge it posed compelled them to maintain a collective position. By working together on the Cambodia issue, ASEAN was able to develop a sense of community and, by the end of the 1980s, the Association had become more than simply a symbol of friendship or a consultative forum.[7] For example, although it preserved its principle of non-intervention in its members' domestic affairs, the decision to hold the third ASEAN Summit in Manila in 1988 was an important recognition of Corazon Aquino's new government. ASEAN had become a community with an identity.

Confidence and Insecurity

In the late 1980s and early 1990s, ASEAN's economies developed markedly, boosting the grouping's confidence. At the same time, the end of the Cold War increased its sense of insecurity. Both developments affected the way in which ASEAN saw itself and the outside world.

Before the late 1980s, the growth of the ASEAN economies had been overshadowed by that of the Newly Industrialised Economies (NIEs) – Hong Kong, South Korea and Taiwan (the other NIE, Singapore, was an ASEAN member). However, the rising value of the Japanese yen against the US dollar from 1985 prompted Japanese firms to look for cheaper production sites overseas, including in the ASEAN states. Direct investment from the NIEs also began to flow into the ASEAN economies; by the early 1990s, NIE investment in ASEAN equalled that of Japan or the US.

Policies introduced by the ASEAN states to take advantage of favourable external conditions were also important in attracting this investment. Economies were partially deregulated, and incentives introduced. Policy shifted from encouraging import-substitution investment to export-oriented investment, allowing the ASEAN states to become exporters of industrial products competing in the markets of industrialised countries. In the wake of the financial crisis of 1997–98, much attention in Europe and the US has focused on the inadequacies of ASEAN's 'crony capitalism'. Some analysts have argued that the lack of individual freedom and transparency made the crises inevitable. However, it is important to remember that, in the late 1980s, regional governments introduced appropriate policies in response to the opportunities which they saw. Much effort went into production, not just speculation. To treat ASEAN's success up to 1997 as no more than a bubble which inevitably burst does not give the whole picture.

Rapid economic growth was seen as proof that ASEAN's aim of national consolidation through development had been achieved, and that its doctrine was therefore infallible. ASEAN's initiatives in

Table 3 *Net Foreign Direct Investment in ASEAN States, 1970, 1980, 1991–1996*

(US$m)	1970	1980	1991	1992	1993	1994	1995	1996
Indonesia	83	180	1,482	1,777	2,004	2,109	4,348	7,960
Laos	0	0	7	8	30	59	88	104
Malaysia	94	934	3,998	5,183	5,006	4,342	4,132	4,500
Myanmar	0	0	238	172	149	91	115	100
Philippines	-25	-106	544	228	1,238	1,591	1,478	1,408
Thailand	43	190	2,014	2,113	1,804	1,366	2,068	2,336
Vietnam	–	–	229	385	523	742	1,400	1,500

Source *Global Development Finance, 1998* (Washington DC: World Bank, 1998)

international relations also seemed to be successful. An increasing number of major powers sent their foreign ministers to PMCs, which acted not only as relatively formal occasions for dialogue with the ASEAN states, but also as a useful neutral ground for bilateral discussions between the officials of non-ASEAN nations. In 1996, Kishore Mahbubani, a senior Singaporean official, wrote that 'only an ASEAN invitation … could draw the major powers to sit together to discuss security matters in the Asia-Pacific because only ASEAN enjoyed the confidence of all the major powers as an impartial organisation'.[8] Whether justified or not, ASEAN's growing confidence signalled a remarkable change from the Association's original role as a defence mechanism against external pressure. ASEAN was beginning to be seen by its members as a source of power and confidence in its own right.

was ASEAN really a source of power?

At the same time, however, the end of the Cold War raised three major challenges for ASEAN, all of which increased the Association's sense of insecurity and encouraged it to strengthen its cohesion. ASEAN was concerned that the fall of the Soviet Union would lead the US to reduce its presence in the region. This fear was not new: it had surfaced in the late 1960s during the Vietnam War, when the Nixon Doctrine called for substantial US force reductions, and had troubled ASEAN thereafter. Cold War or no Cold War, the US presence has remained a key component of ASEAN's balancing strategy in its external relations. When negotiations to extend American use of military bases in the Philippines broke down, prompting Washington to give notice of its complete withdrawal by November 1992, Singapore swiftly agreed to allow US naval vessels and aircraft greater use of its facilities, and also permitted the relocation of a US military logistics facility to its territory. Indonesia and Malaysia also agreed to allow US naval vessels access to their facilities. The US has repeatedly reassured ASEAN that its forward military deployment in East Asia will continue. At the PMC meeting in July 1997, Secretary of State Madeleine Albright outlined the four US interests served by its East Asian presence: security; economics; strategic concerns in a region whose cooperation is needed in responding to threats of proliferation, terrorism, narcotics and environmental damage; and, more problematically for ASEAN, an 'abiding political interest in supporting democracy and respect for human rights and the rule of law, because stability and prosperity ultimately depend on it'.[9] While probably a standard point for a US Secretary of State to make, Albright's last comment demonstrated clearly to ASEAN nations the 'price' of a continuing strong US presence.

The West's apparently tougher post-Cold War line over issues such as human rights and labour conditions posed ASEAN's second challenge. At the ASEAN–European Community (EC) foreign ministers' meeting in September 1991, the Europeans insisted that human rights should be addressed in a new economic-cooperation agreement. In 1992, Jan Pronk, the Dutch minister in charge of economic cooperation, declared that the question of East Timor should be taken up at the long-standing Inter-Governmental Group on Indonesia (IGGI), the international meeting chaired by the Netherlands (as the former colonial ruler) to provide economic aid to Indonesia. ASEAN states, suspecting that they were being punished for being successful, reacted strongly to both developments, believing there to be a hidden agenda behind them. ASEAN's rapid economic growth allowed its members to feel less dependent on economic aid from the industrialised countries. In response to the

East Timor declaration, Indonesia refused the Netherlands the IGGI chair and rejected Dutch aid. The IGGI was dissolved, and replaced by the Consultative Group for Indonesia (CGI), chaired by the World Bank.

The loss of the patron–client relationship with the end of the Cold War also posed problems for non-ASEAN nations such as Japan. But for ASEAN the difficulty was particularly acute since it touched issues of sovereignty – the key to the Association's identity – and because it made it more difficult for ASEAN's members to balance external powers against each other. While the various ASEAN members have differing views on issues such as democracy and human rights, outside pressure in these areas tends to unify their position to fend off 'intrusion' in what are seen as domestic concerns. Indonesia's strong reaction to the Dutch declaration may have been partly prompted by its expectation that the World Bank and Japan would continue to provide aid irrespective of its attitude towards the IGGI. In comparison to these two sources of assistance, Dutch help was negligible. However, ASEAN states cannot assume that similarly favourable circumstances will always be available, and thus cannot rely on continued support regardless of their attitude towards issues such as human rights.

ASEAN's third post-Cold War challenge followed the end of the Cambodian conflict in 1991. The Association's members recognised that the war had engendered a deeper spirit of community between them. Once resolved, and once the communist threat had disappeared, there was therefore a possibility that this new-found cohesion would dissipate. In response, ASEAN members in January 1992 agreed to work towards a Free Trade Area (AFTA). The time was ripe for such an arrangement because economic growth since the late 1980s had increased economic interdependence both in Pacific Asia and, increasingly, in ASEAN itself. ASEAN nations had joined APEC, making it necessary to take steps to prevent the dilution of ASEAN's particular identity. More importantly, in order to survive, ASEAN could no longer simply act as a shield against an external threat that no longer seemed real. The Association needed to find a positive role, and AFTA was seen as the first step on this new road.

ASEAN was in search of a more positive role

Initially, the AFTA proposal envisaged tariffs among ASEAN countries falling to between zero and five per cent within 15 years from January 1993 but, in September 1994, this deadline was brought forward by five years to 2003. The decision to accelerate the reduction timetable was taken two months before the schedule for trade liberalisation in APEC was decided, reflecting the fact that, given its smaller size, AFTA must be a step ahead of APEC in this area if it is to succeed. Some ASEAN states, notably its newer and poorer ones, may, however, find it difficult to meet their albeit more relaxed target of 2008, particularly in the wake of the 1997–98 financial crisis. The crisis may also increase competition between the Association's members for overseas markets and capital, and sharpen intramural disputes over, for example, illegal immigrants and foreign workers. On the other hand, AFTA is expected to be an important tool in maintaining ASEAN's cohesion, and its members are likely to make every effort to safeguard it. If the Association's economic problems are overcome, AFTA will assist in preserving ASEAN's identity.

New Challenges

ASEAN faces a series of new challenges, all of which might have a significant impact on its identity. These include the organisation's expansion to encompass Vietnam in 1995 and Laos and Myanmar in 1997; the effects of the financial crisis; and the reconsideration of the principle of non-intervention triggered by these developments.

Enlarging ASEAN to include all ten South-east Asian countries has long been an objective for its leaders for a variety of reasons. In specific terms, Vietnam's membership may have been especially welcomed by Malaysia and Thailand as a balance to Indonesia in ASEAN; Myanmar's, arranged despite Western criticism, may have been designed to curtail China's influence there, and hence in the wider region. But the underlying importance of enlargement is the desire to unify South-east Asia to ensure its freedom from outside control.

During the Cold War, ASEAN saw itself as a defence against the threat posed by the Association's Indochinese neighbours. Once that threat receded, it seemed natural to embrace these countries, rather than exclude and alienate them. However, enlargement poses some clear problems. First, Myanmar brings with it pressing human-rights issues that are of international concern. This undermines ASEAN's founding aim to prevent outside intervention in the internal affairs of its members. (It is arguable that ASEAN would have found it difficult to tolerate outside intervention in Myanmar irrespective of whether the country was an Association member.)

the economic crisis has divided ASEAN members

Secondly, enlargement has increased ASEAN's political and economic diversity. Given the organisation's principle of consensus, this will make it hard to reach decisions, and the way in which the Association conducts its business may therefore need to change. Modifying the consensus principle would, however, be difficult given that it is the basis on which ASEAN has succeeded in bringing together such a diverse group of countries.

The 1997–98 financial crisis could also have a long-term impact on the Association's unity. The strongly xenophobic tone of complaints about 'foreign speculators', coupled with the International Monetary Fund (IMF)'s stringent policies, may have led some to believe that the crisis would prompt ASEAN states to band more closely together and pursue closed economic cooperation more vigorously. In a bid to defend their currencies and safeguard jobs, ASEAN states have urged their people to refrain from buying foreign goods or undertaking foreign travel, and have tried to deport foreign workers. They have, however, drawn no distinction between their ASEAN partners and other foreign nations. For Malaysia, 'foreign workers' largely meant Indonesians and Filipinos, and, for Thailand, Burmese. These attitudes towards foreign workers raise questions over whether a group of nations can maintain its unity in the face of serious economic crisis, without a framework providing for the free flow of labour and monetary union. Typically, ASEAN has approached this issue cautiously, proposing measures such as surveillance of each other's economies and agreeing, where possible, not to use US dollars for local trade.

Enlargement and the financial crisis have prompted heated debate over the principle of non-intervention, one of the key components of the 'ASEAN way'. The organisation may have to become more willing to exert pressure over the domestic affairs of

Table 4 *ASEAN Macroeconomic Indicators, 1995–1999*

(%)	1995	1996	1997	1998	1999
Indonesia					
GDP growth	8.2	8.0	4.6	-3.0	1.0
Inflation rate	9.5	7.9	6.6	20.0	15.0
Export growth	18.0	5.8	11.2	5.0	7.0
Import growth	26.6	8.1	4.8	-5.0	2.0
Malaysia					
GDP growth	9.5	8.6	7.5	3.5	4.5
Inflation rate	3.4	3.5	4.0	5.0	4.5
Export growth	26.6	7.3	6.0	8.0	10.0
Import growth	30.4	1.7	7.0	6.0	7.0
Philippines					
GDP growth	4.8	5.7	5.1	2.4	4.0
Inflation rate	8.1	8.4	5.1	10.0	8.0
Export growth	29.4	17.7	22.8	21.0	21.0
Import growth	23.7	20.8	14.0	9.0	10.0
Singapore					
GDP growth	8.7	6.9	7.8	3.0	4.5
Inflation rate	1.7	1.4	2.0	3.2	3.3
Export growth	21.0	6.4	-3.1	2.0	4.0
Import growth	21.6	5.4	0.1	2.0	4.0
Thailand					
GDP growth	8.8	5.5	-0.4	-3.0	1.0
Inflation rate	5.8	5.9	5.6	15.0	9.0
Export growth	24.8	-1.9	3.2	5.0	8.0
Import growth	31.9	0.6	-9.3	-15.0	3.0

continued overleaf

Table 4 *ASEAN Macroeconomic Indicators, cont'd*

(%)	1995	1996	1997	1998	1999
Vietnam					
GDP growth	9.5	9.3	9.2	5.0	6.5
Inflation rate	12.7	4.5	3.2	4.0	4.0
Export growth	28.2	41.0	22.2	15.0	16.0
Import growth	43.8	39.0	-1.6	5.0	5.0

Note 1998 and 1999 figures are estimates

Source *Asian Development Outlook 1998* (Oxford: Oxford University Press for the Asian Development Bank, 1998)

some of its members if it is to fend off external intervention. For example, ASEAN is already committed to constructively engaging with Myanmar. While deciding whether to admit Myanmar, ASEAN sought to offset international criticism by undertaking to persuade the regime in Yangon to establish a dialogue with Aung San Suu Kyi's National League for Democracy (NLD). The regime's failure to do so caused acute embarrassment. Similarly, the non-intervention principle was blamed by some for ASEAN's inadequate response to the financial crisis and subsequent political turmoil in Indonesia.

Thailand's proposal at the July 1998 ASEAN meeting that the non-intervention principle should be reviewed, although backed by the Philippines, was reportedly strongly opposed by other members, and no substantive conclusion was reached.[10] Nonetheless, the fact that a debate over the issue took place at all indicates that there is a growing feeling within the organisation that the 'ASEAN way' needs to change to meet altered conditions. At the same time, it demonstrates a growing divergence between countries like Thailand and the Philippines, which have experienced democratisation processes, and those, especially ASEAN's newest members, which have not. The debate over the non-interference principle will remain a test case of ASEAN's ability or willingness to evolve into a closer-knit grouping.

ASEAN has demonstrated how widely diverse countries can create a meaningful community. Begun as a shield against the outside world, its policy of non-intervention, consensus decision-making and developing habits of cooperation has gradually built stability in South-east Asia. ASEAN's members should be proud of this achievement. However, the relevance of the 'ASEAN way' to the wider region is questionable. The ASEAN system already appears inadequate to meet the demands of an enlarged and more diversified membership and the pressures of increased economic inter-dependence, and ASEAN appears to have no desire to expand its role through further enlargement beyond the sub-region. The Association can have a useful regional role because it is not seen as a potentially dominating player. But its lack of resources and over-riding need to maintain its particular identity mean that it will be unable to take a central part in shaping the regional environment.

The 'Asian Way'?

chapter 4

For much of the 1990s, East Asian political leaders, academics and analysts claimed that, despite ethnic, cultural and religious diversity, there was an 'Asian way', and that specifically Asian values existed. These values made the region unique, and proud to be different from 'the West'. Others, while admitting that there was no single set of clearly defined values applicable to Asia as a whole, or even to East Asia, suggested that at least *some* common ground existed. To justify their position, many 'Asian-values' proponents cited South-east Asia's dramatic economic development in the early 1990s, and argued that East Asian dynamism would be the defining feature of the twenty-first century. Despite East Asia's difficulties in uniting as a community, the region's states could and would prosper as a group, not only economically, but also as a civilisation.

By the end of the 1990s, the Asian-values debate seems an embarrassing irrelevance.[1] Western critics exploited the financial crisis of 1997–98 to vindicate their own position, and to support their case that the West's values had triumphed over those of Asia. The crisis has prompted a greater recognition in East Asia that the region's economies are part of a global system, and cannot prosper alone; boastful claims of the merits of the 'Asian way' may as a result become less frequent. However, the values debate remains important because the social and psychological conditions on which it is based persist. As Kishore Mahbubani puts it, 'The Asian mind, having been awakened, cannot be put to sleep'.[2]

The Asian-values debate encompasses a wide variety of interpretations and points of view, exemplified by the profusion of terms through which it is conducted – 'Asian way', 'Asian values', 'Asianism', 'Pacific way' and 'Asia-Pacific fusion', for example. Sweeping statements identifying Asian values as essentially Confucian or as emphasising the centrality of the family are inadequate. Similarly, it is not sufficient simply to label the advocates of Asian values as critics of the problems of modern, industrial society, or as trying to justify the rule of Asia's political élites. The views of so-called 'Asian way' adherents are diverse, and sometimes even mutually exclusive; the single common thread appears to be a pride in being Asian. Nonetheless, it is possible to identify three broad lines of Asianist argument, based on economics, politics and 'civilisation'. Particularly in the wake of the financial crisis, too much emphasis has been placed on economic issues, and too little on the political or civilisational aspects of the debate, both of which have far greater implications.

an awakened Asian mind 'cannot be put to sleep'

The Economic Argument

Given the dramatic rise and subsequent crisis of the East Asian economies in the 1990s, it is not surprising that both proponents and critics of the concept of Asian values have been preoccupied with its relevance to economic success. However, for the defenders of Asian values, using economic success to prove the merit of their case raises three problems. First, it implies that these values have worth, not so much in their own right, but rather in the extent to which they benefit economies. Using economic growth as a yardstick entails applying Western measures of success such as gross domestic product (GDP) to what are seen as uniquely Asian concepts. Proponents of Asian values would perhaps do better to use standards more in keeping with Asian culture, such as the extent to which social harmony or 'harmony with nature' is increased. The second set of problems stems from the question of whether Asian values or Asian ways can be said to have triumphed over Western ones given that no Asian economy employing uniquely Asian practices has outstripped either the EU or the US. Japan is the possible exception, but it is not clear whether important features of its economy – good labour relations, egalitarian pay structures and sophisticated quality-control techniques – are traditionally 'Asian', or even traditionally Japanese. The type of government-led economic management typical of Asia is by no means unique to the region. The third problem with this argument is that it is virtually impossible to identify a common East Asian or even South-east Asian set of values that could account for the region's economic development, given the diversity of its styles and levels between countries. It is thus futile to pose questions such as 'Does a Confucian education or an emphasis on the importance of the family contribute to development?' because no non-economic factor can convincingly explain economic success in any one country, let alone in different states. It is odd that Confucianism is now mentioned as one of the keys to South-east Asia's economic growth two decades after it was used to explain why the region lagged behind Hong Kong, South Korea and Taiwan.

East Asia's economic success in the early 1990s did little, therefore, to prove the worth of Asian values but, by the same token, the financial crisis of 1997–98 did little to disprove it. Rapid economic growth was due mainly to foreign direct investment prompted on the one hand by changes in the international economic situation, among them the rising yen, and on the other by the appropriate economic policies of recipient countries. Similarly, the financial crisis was also largely due to international economic changes, including the rising value of the US dollar, and to policy mistakes, such as an excessive pegging of currencies to the dollar and a failure to ensure proper regulation of financial institutions. Throughout these changes, the nature of East Asia's societies remained relatively constant. There are issues that need to be addressed in the context of the economic debate, among them the extent to which 'crony capitalism' and other transparency problems hinder East Asia's long-term development. But cronyism, although in some ways associated with respect for the family, has not been identified as an Asian value. In terms of the debate over what made South-east Asia's economic rise possible, and what caused its later crisis, many Asians and Westerners alike view the Asian-values debate as both irrelevant and a distraction.

The Political Argument

The debate over Asian values also has a political dimension. As a result of rapid economic growth, East Asians who had 'struggled with the subconscious assumption that perhaps they were second-rate' came to believe that they could match the West, both individually and as nations.[3] They gained the confidence to compare their societies on an equal footing with those of the West. In doing so, they saw aspects of the West's political culture that they admired, such as openness in argument and the accountability of public officials.[4] For Malaysia's former Deputy Prime Minister Anwar Ibrahim, for example, development 'can only be achieved in a liberal, free environment, and that builds a need for democracy and civil society'.[5]

East Asia's leaders also saw features of the West that they did not like, such as illegal drug use and violent crime, which they interpreted as symptoms of the 'breakdown of civil society'.[6] Although social problems similar to the West's are growing in East Asia, and confidence has been dented by the financial crisis, Asians are now less likely uncritically to accept Western ways and values as their model. For proponents of the 'Asian way', economic progress should not entail sacrificing their values, nor developing the problems that they see in Western societies. As former Thai Prime Minister Anand Panyarachun puts it, it is in no one's interest to 'attempt to remake others in their image, as the only response will be resistance'.[7]

This defensive aspect of the Asian-values argument is part of the region's long-standing attempts to preserve its distinctiveness from the West. While Thais and Filipinos, who have fought for and won more liberal political systems, may have opinions on issues such as democracy and the rights of the individual that differ from those held in other South-east Asian states, there is still a conviction that room should be made for divergent cultures and values between nations and, more widely, between East Asia and the West. The view that the West should not be allowed to meddle in the internal affairs of the region's states is shared, not just by their political élites, but also by their people. In mid-1997, soon after the financial crisis began, Malaysian Prime Minister Mahathir Mohamad blamed 'foreign speculators' for deliberately creating it. In countries needing IMF

room should be made for divergent cultures

help – Indonesia, South Korea and Thailand – public resentment grew over the stringent conditions attached to assistance and the hardship that they caused.

However, despite the popularity of books with titles such as *The Japan (or the China) That Can Say 'No'*, this defensive attitude has not had a decisive policy impact. Although Mahathir has suggested that only Asian states should be allowed membership of his mooted East Asia Economic Caucus (EAEC), thereby excluding Australia, Japan has insisted that the EAEC would be unacceptable without Australia and New Zealand. Singapore, which has produced the most vocal Asian-values proponents, has also been one of the strongest advocates of a robust US presence in East Asia, and appeared sympathetic to Japan's oft-repeated proposal to include Australia and New Zealand in ASEM. In Japan itself, the positive economic and political changes taking place in neighbouring states have generally been seen as part of an inevitable progression towards Western values. Following the end of the Cold War, Japan identified itself more closely, not less, with key Western principles. Finally, the first-ever meeting between the leaders of ASEAN, China, South Korea and Japan in December 1997 did not become the high-profile protest against the West's response to the financial crisis that might have been expected given the volume of anti-Western rhetoric at home. Thus, with the possible exception of Malaysia, the Asian-values argument has not dictated East Asia's policy agenda.

The Civilisation Argument

By relying on economic or political arguments, both critics and proponents assumed a timeless difference between Asian values and those of the West, and ignored the social and political changes under way in both Asian and Western societies. As a result, both camps tended to emphasise their differences, rather than attempt to resolve them. This approach was, however, inadequate for those in East Asia who sought, or already enjoyed, principles perceived to be Western, such as liberal democracy, while at the same time remaining convinced of the significance of Asian civilisation.

One answer to this problem was to argue that these seemingly Western values had also been part of Asian thinking, thereby making it wrong to claim that liberal democracy was alien to Asia. One could be both a believer in Asian values, and a liberal democrat.

This approach also made it possible to counter those in the West who argued that Western ways needed to be accepted wholesale in order to make liberal democracy possible. Figures frequently cited in the context of this type of argument include Sun Yat-sen and the nineteenth and twentieth-century Indian poet Rabindrinath Tagore, together with older thinkers such as Meng-tzu, and the ideas of Korea's native religion, Tonghok.[8] Since the basic ideas for democracy already existed in Asia, the fact that modern democratic systems were developed elsewhere did not automatically mean that they would not succeed in Asia.[9]

The work of two US writers, Francis Fukuyama and Samuel Huntington, made this synthesising project more urgent. Fukuyama's *The End of History and the Last Man*, published in 1992, broadly argued that, with the end of the Cold War, Western civilisation had triumphed, and that all others including Asia's would inevitably wither away.[10] Huntington's thesis, which first emerged in 1993, suggested that, while Asian civilisation would survive, at least for the time being, it would inevitably come into conflict with the West.[11] These views have met with two basic responses. The first, and in some ways most appealing, rebuttal is based on the simple belief that confrontation is not inevitable, and that coexistence is possible. The second and more complex response is to argue that, through the constant contact between Asia and the West, the two civilisations will eventually fuse to form a third possessing the best aspects of its antecedents. In a similar way, Western civilisation can be seen as itself the result of this type of fusion – an accretion of Greek, Roman, Islamic and other influences. Thus, Kazuo Ogura argues that 'Asia should now thoroughly absorb what the West has offered and develop a new set of values that it can transmit to the world'.[12] The nature of the 'new' civilisation emerging from this fusion has been variously described as strongly Asian (Kishore Mahbubani's 'Pacific way'), relatively Western (Yoichi Funabashi's 'Asia-Pacific fusion') or 'Westernistic'.[13]

on the road to becoming Westernistic?

In the wake of East Asia's financial crisis, Western critics seem overly preoccupied with the apparent failure of the economic argument to prove the merit of Asian values. The political and civilisational aspects of the debate will, however, have the greatest implications for the development of East Asia's identity. For some, the concept of Asian values justifies distancing Asia from the West; the defensive element of the political argument will thus be a significant constraint to Asia establishing an open, comprehensive relationship with the rest of the world. For others, the civilisation argument, with its concept of fusion, may hold out the prospect of a new relationship, and may make it possible for East Asia to merge with an Asia-Pacific world, while preserving its distinct identity. The following chapter assesses the success of attempts to create such an 'Asia-Pacific community'.

chapter 5

An Asia-Pacific Community?

In the 1990s, much of the rhetoric concerning economic and security relations in East Asia has involved reference to the Asia-Pacific, rather than simply to Asia. Two speeches delivered 20 years apart make the point. In an address in Manila marking ASEAN's tenth anniversary in 1977, then Japanese Prime Minister Takeo Fukuda used the word 'Asia' exclusively when seeking to identify himself or his country with his audience. In a speech given in Singapore by Hashimoto in 1997, marking ASEAN's thirtieth anniversary, the Prime Minister used the term 'Asia' three times, and 'Asia-Pacific' more than ten.[1] Both speeches were delivered to an ASEAN audience, and both had a similar purpose; Hashimoto even made reference to Fukuda's address. But the differences in language demonstrate how important the idea of the 'Asia-Pacific' has become, even in a dialogue exclusively involving East Asians. Those of the fusion school are optimistic about the prospects for Asia-Pacific cooperation. Their optimism may, however, be misplaced: while the vision of an Asia-Pacific community may be more than a chimera, its outlines remain unclear.[2]

Asia-Pacific Cooperation

Discussions of Asia-Pacific cooperation began in the 1960s, but became substantive in the 1970s following a series of changes which called for new thinking. Although the Nixon Doctrine of 1969 and the strategic *rapprochement* between the US and China forced the region to develop new strategies, arguably of more importance was the UK's withdrawal of forces 'East of Suez' in the late 1960s, and its decision to join the European Economic Community (EEC), which it did in 1973. London's closer economic relationship with its Western European partners prompted Commonwealth countries in the Pacific, particularly Australia and New Zealand, to look closer to home for new markets for their primary products. By 1967, Japan had become Australia's largest export market, while Australia had become a vital source of raw materials such as iron ore and coal crucial to Japan's economic development. Both countries also shared an ambivalent attitude towards their identities: Japan, with its roots in Asia, had adopted Western values; Australia, with its roots in Europe, was seeking a new Pacific identity. Since 1972, Australia and Japan have held regular ministerial-level meetings and, during the 1970s and 1980s, the two countries became the leading players in the Asia-Pacific cooperation process. Initially at least, Pacific cooperation was driven by the region's developed nations, and aimed at securing US attention and increased stability in South-east Asia; the region itself was probably seen more as a subject for cooperation than as a participant in it.

The differing perspectives of the developed states, such as Australia and Japan, and those of South-east Asia were highlighted in September 1980, when a seminar on the 'Pacific community', supported by Australia and Japan, was held in Canberra. Attended by government officials, academics and business people from 12 countries and regions, the seminar later developed into the Pacific Economic Cooperation Council (PECC). Although there was general support at the seminar for setting up a framework to discuss economic cooperation in the Pacific at government level, ASEAN participants were reluctant to push the initiative too far. By 1980, the Association's members had begun work related to the Cambodian conflict, and PMCs with dialogue partners had started. The organisation was, however, still in the process of building a common identity, and feared that participation in a multilateral framework might undermine these efforts and weaken ASEAN's ability to fend off outside influences. The Association was also wary of becoming entangled in a special relationship with the West which would compromise its neutral stance, making it more difficult to play off outside powers against each other. The PECC agreed at the Canberra seminar took these concerns into account by retaining its non-governmental status and emphasising confidence-building through informal contacts and personal relationships. Its basic mode of conduct was therefore similar to that of ASEAN.

The second important development in Pacific cooperation took place in January 1989, when Australia proposed the APEC forum; the first ministerial meeting was held in November that year.[3] APEC was formed in response to a number of Australian and Japanese concerns, including increased conflicts over Pacific trade, particularly between Japan and the US, which threatened greater unilateralism and exclusive bilateralism, and a feeling that GATT's Uruguay Round had stalled, jeopardising the international trading system. In addition, the prospect of closer European economic cooperation and the increasing likelihood of a North American free-trade zone prompted the other Asia-Pacific states to look for stronger regional trade ties. These ties would be all the more important if the Uruguay Round failed completely.

the motive for APEC and the challenge to ASEAN

ASEAN cautiously accepted the APEC proposal. The Association's members shared Australian and Japanese concerns over the state of international trade relations, while the organisation's changed view of itself was probably also important in prompting its participation. By the end of the 1980s, ASEAN had become more confident about its common identity and the strength of its individual members. Moreover, the transition to export-driven economies fuelled by direct foreign investment meant that the Association felt the need to keep developed countries engaged in order to secure access to their markets, and to compete with new rivals for direct investment, such as China and Europe's former-communist states. They could not, therefore, afford to turn down the APEC proposal.

Nonetheless, ASEAN countries remained apprehensive that participation in APEC risked ceding control to outside powers. They thus made specific proposals of their own to prevent APEC from weakening the Association's sense of unity. These were:

- that ASEAN would take primary responsibility for administering APEC's ministerial meetings;

Table 5 *APEC Members, 1997*

	Population (m)	GDP (US$bn)	GDP per head (US$)
Australia	18.53	394	21,248
Brunei	0.29	5	17,246
Canada	30.29	618	20,389
Chile	14.62	77	5,273
China	1,243.74	918	740
Hong Kong SAR	6.50	172	26,499
Indonesia	200	215	1,066
Japan	125.64	4,193	33,222
Malaysia	21	98	4,544
Mexico	96.40	403	4,231
New Zealand	3.76	65	17,317
Papua New Guinea	4.21	5	946
Peru	24.37	65	2,676
Philippines	73	82	1,118
Russia	147.10	450	3,045
Singapore	3	96	25,754
South Korea	45.99	443	9,623
Taiwan	21.68	283	13,070
Thailand	60.60	154	2,540
US	267.90	8,080	30,160
Vietnam	76.55	26	335

Note   SAR = Special Administrative Region

Sources   APEC Secretariat, www.apecsec.org; *World Development Report, 1998/99*
(New York: Oxford University Press for the World Bank, 1998)

- that the different levels of economic and political development within the APEC states should be taken into consideration; and
- that APEC should be a forum for constructive discussion, not a mechanism to enforce action by its members.

Some of these proposals were accepted, others not. ASEAN was compelled to give most ground at the outset on the format of APEC meetings. At the first ministerial gathering in Canberra, it was agreed that the second meeting would be held in Singapore, but the third in non-ASEAN Seoul. Thereafter, venues would alternate between ASEAN and non-ASEAN states. The Association's views on the appropriate mode of discussion won greater support, and it was agreed that diversity in levels of economic development would be taken into account, that decisions would be reached by consensus, and that emphasis would be placed on an informal, frank exchange of views. Thus, APEC's procedures resembled those of PECC and ASEAN itself.

In its early years, APEC developed quietly. Non-ASEAN members were sensitive to the need to make the Association feel comfortable in the multilateral framework that it had reluctantly entered. APEC's initial projects, most of which were proposed by Japan and South Korea, were designed to be innocuous yet appealing to ASEAN. They included initiatives such as trade and investment data reviews, trade promotion, investment and technology transfers and developing human resources. APEC's symmetrical composition – six ASEAN states and six non-ASEAN ones – gave the relatively cosy if inaccurate impression of APEC as a forum in which dialogue partners cooperated with the Association.

This arrangement became less comfortable in 1991, when China, Hong Kong and Taiwan were admitted to APEC. All three were important regional traders, and had been members of the PECC since 1986. They were not, however, ASEAN dialogue partners, while China was a direct competitor for outside assistance. ASEAN states were becoming a minority, a process accelerated by the admission of Mexico and Papua New Guinea in 1993, Chile in 1994 and Peru and Russia in 1998.

More importantly, the content of discussion was beginning to change. At the APEC meeting in Seattle in November 1993, the US took advantage of its position as chair to establish trade liberalisation as the forum's major objective, and to propose creating an Asia-Pacific community. The timing of the move was important, since the US Congress had given Washington until 15 December 1993 to resolve the bilateral issues with the EU that had stalled GATT's Uruguay Round. Washington thus may have wanted to strengthen its Pacific links against the EU.[4] The administration had also adopted a longer-term strategy to engage seriously with the Asia-Pacific. This new US enthusiasm increased concern in China and in some ASEAN countries, notably Malaysia, that APEC would become a rigid, US-dominated institution. Since 1993, trade liberalisation has overwhelmed the US-led agenda. However, to ease Chinese and ASEAN fears, the US conceded that APEC could not be used to negotiate a binding agreement. As a result, liberalisation was framed in Individual Action Plans (IAPs) submitted by members themselves. IAPs were designed to 'achieve free and open trade and investment in the Asia Pacific region by the year 2010 for developed economies and 2020 for developing economies'. The APEC Economic Leaders' Declaration in November 1997 noted that 'trade and investment liberalisation' was not the forum's sole aim, but rather one of its 'three mutually supportive pillars', along with 'business facilitation' and 'economic and technical cooperation'.[5]

APEC's identity is reshaped by non-ASEAN members

The November 1997 Declaration concluded by claiming that 'Through a combination of concrete results and renewed vision, the spirit of community which unites us has been strengthened and broadened'. However, APEC must overcome several challenges before it can claim to be a community with a common identity. APEC was set up as a proactive forum, and cannot thrive simply as a 'friendly group' of nations. On the other hand, it must find the right pace and type of activity if it is to avoid alienating any of its members.

A particular problem, which has been a sensitive issue from the beginning, concerns APEC members' divergent views of the appropriate pace of trade liberalisation. This is not simply a question of Asians being less enthusiastic than the East Pacific nations;

Singapore has always keenly supported liberalisation, and, as the APEC chair, Indonesia played a leading role in setting its timetable in 1994. Nonetheless, changes already implemented have placed a strain on ASEAN, and on APEC as a whole. This became apparent at the meetings held in Manila in 1998, when APEC could barely hide its internal divisions over the question of trade liberalisation. At the same time, the US needs to maintain the pace of liberalisation in order to preserve domestic support for APEC.

Enlarging APEC also poses challenges. With both China and Russia included, APEC's political significance has considerably increased. While the forum is designed to deal only with economic issues, it can thus also play a political role: the Seattle meeting provided an opportunity for Clinton and Jiang to meet for the first time after Tiananmen without provoking overly strong opposition. China and Russia are not members of the WTO; the opportunities APEC affords for engaging these nations in a multilateral economic framework should not therefore be underrated. But some APEC members can see these merits as challenges. Russian membership may be viewed as the start of APEC's domination by the major powers, while the economic needs of the forum's new states may distract attention away from those of older members. Concerns such as these may be felt, not only by the ASEAN states, but also by medium-sized powers such as Australia and South Korea. An enlarged membership has also meant that the natural affinities between the members and their economic interdependence have declined.

Despite these obstacles, APEC can be expected to continue to develop given the important national interests at stake for its members. For economies outside the North American Free Trade Agreement (NAFTA), APEC is crucial to ensuring a continued US presence and interest in the region. The alternative means of achieving this – extending NAFTA to selected countries in East Asia – has supporters in South Korea and Singapore, but would fragment the network of production established in East Asia by businesses from Japan and the NIEs, and would be damaging to those states not admitted. Similarly, a transatlantic free-trade agreement between the US and the EU would pose considerable problems for East Asian economies in the absence of APEC.[6] For the US, APEC has been the most cost-effective way of promoting trade and investment liberalisation in the Asia-Pacific. The slowdown in the region's economic growth after 1997 has only marginally undermined Washington's interest in APEC. Politically, APEC offers a useful opportunity for the US to engage with Russia, China and Japan at head-of-state and government level. This is particularly important in the case of those countries with which bilateral relations are prone to strain.

The East Asia Economic Caucus

While APEC has established the Asia-Pacific as a meaningful concept, other groupings partly overlap with it, or are separate from it. Some are the product of economic motives, but others are related to questions of identity. APEC is in some senses in competition with another initiative, the EAEC. The EAEC is a diluted version of the East Asian Economic Group (EAEG), put forward by Malaysian Prime Minister Mahathir in 1990, which was designed to encompass both ASEAN and North-east Asian countries. Mahathir made his proposal abruptly and without detail, with little or no consultation with his ASEAN partners and in the peculiar setting of a visit to China. As a result, it met with a mixed reception from the Association's other members. Moreover, since the mooted grouping included China, Japan and South Korea as well as the ASEAN states, it risked weakening, rather than enhancing, the Association's cohesion.

Despite these concerns, the EAEG may have had an economic rationale. By liberalising trade between ASEAN and North-east Asia, the Association could have offered an improved investment climate not only to Japan and South Korea, but also to other states outside the grouping. However, the US – for many East Asian states a, if not the, primary export destination – strongly opposed the initiative, which it believed would weaken APEC. As a result, 'Caucus' replaced 'Group' in a bid to make the proposal seem less exclusive. It became more a consultation forum within APEC, rather than an economic grouping in competition with it. This change in nomenclature did not, however, placate the US or Australia, both of which maintained that such a coterie within APEC would divide the organisation and was therefore not desirable. While this argument did not convince EAEC advocates, since similar criticisms could be levelled against both NAFTA and the Closer Economic Relations (CER) agreement between Australia and New Zealand, they appear to have dropped references to a Caucus in favour of ad hoc meetings with the foreign ministers of China, Japan and South Korea. Such meetings, dubbed 'ASEAN plus three', have been held during PMCs since 1994.

The EAEG proposal was also problematic for Japan. When it was mooted, Japan was in the process of redefining its relations with the US and East Asia after the end of the Cold War. Many politicians and business people supported Mahathir's proposal precisely because the US opposed it. However, the economic benefits of joining the grouping were unclear. First, the EAEG threatened to undermine attempts to keep the US connected to East Asia. Second, it was not a large enough arena for the Japanese economy, which thrived in the global trading system. Creating a closed economic bloc was unacceptable, and would undermine what had been achieved by decades of global free trade. Japan was also sensitive to Canberra's concerns over the apparently racial overtones of Mahathir's proposed membership criteria, which excluded Australia and New Zealand. Despite East Asia's economic development, Tokyo was still unique in the region in terms of its economic weight, its position as a major provider of overseas assistance and source of capital flows. Bringing Australia and New Zealand into the fold would have freed the group from a donor–recipient type of framework, and could possibly have opened up the discussion, as was the case in APEC, in which all members met as equal partners.

By contrast, China was one of the first countries to support the EAEG proposal, although Beijing never became its enthusiastic promoter. At the ASEAN plus three summit in December 1997, Jiang Zemin is reported to have spoken of 'making the best use of the existing mechanism', and the Chinese spokesman made clear that Beijing saw no link between ASEAN plus three and the EAEC.[7] China's qualified support may have been due both to the fact that Mahathir made his proposal during a visit to China, and to the fact that China was not at the time a member of APEC.

While some argue that the EAEG proposal was instrumental in prompting the US to take APEC seriously as a bridge between itself and East Asia, Mahathir's initiative failed to unite the countries of the region. Although the development of investment and trade networks in the 1990s made consultation between East Asian states useful, it did not make the case for a formal grouping such as the EAEG. However, consultation and cooperation on economic issues may increase in the wake of the 1997–98 crisis, which further emphasised to East Asians both the extent to which their economies were interconnected, and the need *the case for the* for collective responses to the serious *EAEG remains weak* problems the crisis created. The initial funding for Thailand's July 1997 financial-adjustment package was provided not only by Japan ($4bn) and South Korea ($500m), but also by Australia and China, which each pledged $1bn. As analyst Richard Higgot put it, 'In their own ways, all states were attempting to consolidate regional positions in both an economic (de facto) and political (de jure) fashion'.[8]

The ASEAN Regional Forum

While the economic institutions mentioned above can at least claim to be trying to build a community or a shared identity in East Asia, the same cannot be said of the ARF, the region's only multilateral security framework. The Forum was formally proposed by ASEAN and endorsed by its dialogue partners at the PMC in July 1993. (Japan had made a similar proposal to the PMC two years earlier, but this was turned down by ASEAN and the US as premature.) The first working session of ARF foreign ministers – comprising ASEAN, its dialogue partners and Russia, China, Papua New Guinea, Vietnam and Laos – was held in July 1994. Cambodia, India, Mongolia and Myanmar had joined by 1998.

While the need for a multilateral arrangement had increased with the end of the Cold War, from the outset there was no intention of the ARF becoming a 'community' similar to APEC, or of it supplanting security relations based on bilateral arrangements. The US and China, the region's two most important security players, both firmly believed in their versions of bilateral relations centring on themselves ('hub and spoke' in the case of the US, and a 'concentric relationship' in the case of China). Both Washington and Beijing were thus suspicious of any multilateral arrangement that did not have them at its core. Regional countries benefiting from these bilateral relationships – notably Japan and South Korea, but also most ASEAN members – were similarly wary of reducing the importance of their security ties with outside powers. The ARF was thus initially designed as a second-tier arrangement supplementing the region's bilateral links, and acting as a mechanism through which its members could notify each other of developments in security relations. Michael Leifer suggests that 'the ARF's structural problem is that its viability seems to depend on the prior existence of a stable balance, but it is not in a position to create it'.[9] However, this is precisely how the ARF was first envisaged. ASEAN secured the prominence that it desired, and deliberately moulded the forum in its own image. As Leifer puts it, 'the ASEAN model conspicuously avoided the problem of power by addressing regional security on a cooperative basis'.[10]

In APEC's case, ASEAN had failed to assert its claim to be the leading body within the forum. However, its views towards the ARF prevailed. Like the PMCs, ARF meetings would be held in conjunction with the Association's Foreign Ministers' Meetings. There are several possible explanations for why ASEAN compromised over APEC, but not over the ARF. The Association may have been relatively confident of preserving its economic identity within APEC, but less certain of itself in security matters. APEC's perceived domination by the US in 1993 may also have made ASEAN more determined to push through its preferred vision of the ARF.

Whatever the reasons behind it, ASEAN's insistence on retaining the central role within the ARF introduced a further factor affecting the Forum's scope of action and its potential to develop a sense of community among its members. In positive terms, the ARF's promotion by ASEAN, rather than by the US or Japan alone, made it easier for China to consider participating; ASEAN's insistence that

ASEAN stunts ARF growth

progress within the ARF should be gradual was shared by Beijing.[11] However, ASEAN's centrality to the ARF has also created limitations. While the forum is often said, like APEC, to follow the ASEAN model, there are important differences. Like ASEAN, APEC's form has tried to prevent any one member from dominating the agenda. Instead, members take turns as equals in the chair, and the more powerful have to exercise at least formal restraint, as did Indonesia in ASEAN. This has given APEC the potential to build a community among its member-states. By contrast, the ARF is limited to a security-related version of the PMCs whose form it mirrors. As a result, the limitations of the PMCs are also those of the ARF: non-ASEAN dialogue partners have little sense of being shareholders in the grouping, and, while 'intersessional groups' of high-level officials on specific subjects are useful since they are flexible in chairmanship and venue, they cannot outweigh the limitations of the ministerial meeting. Second, while the ARF has decided to move gradually from confidence-building to preventive diplomacy and, ultimately, conflict-resolution, it seems unlikely that issues not of direct concern to ASEAN will be addressed seriously as long as the ARF remains the *ASEAN* Regional Forum. The extent to which the ARF can develop will depend largely on how confident and open-minded ASEAN can be about both its identity and its relations with multilateral institutions.

The Asia–Europe Meeting

ASEM, which was proposed by Singapore in October 1994, added a new dimension to relations between East Asia and the outside world. Its first meeting, bringing together heads of state or government from 25 Asian and European countries and the European Commission, was held in Bangkok in March 1996. In economic, political and security terms, the weakest link in the triangular relationship between Asia, North America and Europe has been that between Europe and Asia. On one level, ASEM is thus an attempt to strengthen this link. On another, however, it has a particular meaning for ASEAN countries, many of which are former European colonies, because it provides a special opportunity for them to treat with Europeans as equals at head-of-state or government level. While Thailand maintained its independence throughout the colonial period, Thai Prime Minister Banharn Silpa-Archa's reference at the first ASEM meeting to 'reconnecting Asia and Europe' can be seen as a reflection of this general view of ASEM within ASEAN.

Another important aim of ASEM may have been to counterbalance what ASEAN saw as APEC's unwelcome tendency to be dominated by the US, whose idea of 'open regionalism' did not, in fact, seem very open at all. It was hoped that, 'just as APEC was a way to help keep the Europeans committed to open multilateralism, so a closer Euro-Asian dialogue could maintain Washington's commitment to open multilateralism and more equal partnership with allies'.[12] Furthermore, ASEAN's defensive instinct made it wary of ties to a single outside power. Thus, ASEM's success might demonstrate that East Asia need not be confined to APEC, but could forge independent links with Europe.

ASEM's future raises two main questions. First, can it develop into a community similar to that which APEC intends itself to be? While there is a great deal on which Asia and Europe can cooperate, ASEM's emphasis is on developing a good working partnership, rather than a community. Developments in ASEM may feed into APEC (as well as into the WTO) and vice versa, but ASEM is neither an alternative nor even a competitor to APEC. Second, has East Asia's sense of identity been strengthened now that its states have shown themselves able to work together outside the Asia-Pacific context?[13] It is doubtful whether East Asia's nations are moving smoothly towards a view of themselves as one entity. When ASEM's Asian members sought to choose a coordinator, North-east Asians rejected ASEAN's idea that one coordinator should be 'for' the Association, another 'for' the other Asian states. Instead, while an ASEAN and a non-ASEAN coordinator were chosen, neither explicitly acted for each grouping. Although curbed, ASEAN's insistence on maintaining its independence was thus again evident.

Despite APEC's commitment to deepening the spirit of community between its members, competing identities and fora mean that the potential viability of the Asia-Pacific as a unifying identity remains unclear. For countries like Australia, Japan and possibly, to an increasing degree, South Korea, all of whom look both to East Asia and to the West for their sense of identity, the Asia-Pacific is a comfortable environment, and cooperation there a goal which they have pursued for many years. For other APEC members, national interests may be more of a spur than questions of identity. The forum's ability to create a sense of community between its members has been undermined by the emergence of cross-cutting groupings, ASEAN's insistence on maintaining its particular identity and the need to retain US engagement. Other developments may further complicate the environment for cooperation. Many analysts have stressed the importance of a so-called 'soft regionalism' based on economic and business links, exemplified by, for example, the Chinese Economic Area (CEA) comprising China, Hong Kong and Taiwan; a looser 'Greater China' or 'Chinese Network'; or the Japanese business network. Together with the region's several 'growth triangles', the most well-known of which is probably that between Singapore, Johor in Malaysia and Riau in Indonesia, this soft regionalism has been expected to change East Asian economies 'from dependency to self-reliance'.[14]

As APEC continues to develop, its spirit of community may grow, as APEC leaders urge and some analysts predict. 'Asia-Pacific' has been firmly established as a useful – even politically correct – concept. But it is not yet clear whether APEC's diverse members share a similar definition of what 'Asia-Pacific' means, or how strongly nations identify with it, rather than with other concepts such as East Asia. 'Asia-Pacific fusion' may be an attractive idea, but it has yet to win general support.

Since the Second World War, the larger North-east Asian countries have tended to lack the strong leadership needed to build a community in East Asia, while the relatively weaker South-east Asian states, although willing to engage in institution-building, have staunchly insisted on their own, specific 'ASEAN-centricity'. In addition, East Asians have not succeeded in resolving the tension between the overriding need to keep the US engaged in the region, and the desire to establish an (East) Asian identity. As a result, the process of community-building has been slow.

The responsibility for ensuring stability in East Asia lies largely with Japan and China, the region's most significant powers. Neither country has, however, been willing or able to shoulder this burden. By contrast, South-east Asian states have, despite their diversity and many disagreements, come together to fend off outside influences. Their common endeavours over the Cambodian conflict in the 1980s, together with the rapid economic growth of the late 1980s and early 1990s, gave ASEAN members a sense of confidence and unity, making possible the Association's transformation from a defensive shield to a source of pride and power in its own right.

This transformation has not, however, been taken to its full extent. ASEAN has participated in multilateral fora such as APEC, and has proposed others such as the ARF. On the other hand, the Association has continued to resist diluting its particular identity within these groupings. ASEAN's long-standing practice of balancing outside powers against each other has persisted. As a result,

ASEAN has demonstrated how diverse nations can build a common identity and achieve stability and peace without tying members to formal unification. But at the same time, ASEAN's need to safeguard its newly acquired identity has led it to shy away from exporting this 'ASEAN way' to the wider region of East Asia or the Asia-Pacific. The greater diversity that enlargement will bring and the effects of the financial crisis are likely to make the Association's defensive instincts even more resistant to change.

Japan's challenge has been to involve itself in Asia, particularly in political and security matters, without causing concern either at home or abroad. The 1990s have seen developments in this direction. As the sub-regional distinctions within East Asia have blurred, Japan has sought to redefine its identity, both in terms of its past, and of its post-war values such as pacifism and human rights. This

Japan's burdens and responsibilities

process has compelled Japan to face Asia more squarely, and has increased the country's self-assurance. As a result, it may become more willing to take the initiative in political and security, as well as economic, areas.

Working with others in a regional framework poses a more complex challenge for China. Nationalism based on its self-image as a victimised developing nation has become more important as communism's position as the country's unifying ideology has eroded. At the same time, China's overlapping identity as a great world power has been strengthened by the world's growing recognition of its market's enormous potential. The combination of these two perceptions has led Beijing to try to change the status quo in a forceful way. In the early part of the 1990s, China resembled the very nineteenth-century colonial powers that it had criticised so strongly in the past. By the decade's close, the country is increasingly willing to act as a responsible world power seeking stable relations in a multipolar world. A key test of this transformation will be Beijing's treatment of the Taiwan question.

The way in which both Japan and China see themselves as stabilising powers is based on their respective relations with the US. Japan considers itself a link between East Asia and the West; the Japan–US security arrangements 'serve as a sort of infrastructure for stability and economic prosperity in the Asia-Pacific'.¹ China's preferred view of itself – as a responsible world power – is linked to a strategic partnership with the US. Each country views with concern the other's relationship with Washington. For Japan, strengthened US ties with China raise fears that its own relationship may become more distant, and that its role as liaison between the US and East Asia may come under pressure. On the other hand, China's past makes it suspicious of Japan–US ties. Progress has been made on this issue, such as the trilateral security meetings first convened in July 1998, but it remains to be seen whether initiatives such as this can make positive contributions to East Asia's security environment.

In the meantime, the most pressing task is revitalising East Asia's economies. A return to prosperity would encourage China's reform and opening process; lessen Japan's introspection; make disagreements between the South-east Asian states less acute; and allow the Asia-Pacific region as a whole to move beyond both the triumphalism of the East Pacific, and the resentment of the West. The prospects of achieving these goals depend to an enormous extent on Japan's ability to reform and return to growth.

The Framework of Regional Cooperation in the Asia-Pacific

	ASEAN	ARF	PMC	APEC	PECC	ASEM
Brunei	❖	❖	❖	❖	❖	❖
Indonesia	❖	❖	❖	❖	❖	❖
Malaysia	❖	❖	❖	❖	❖	❖
Philippines	❖	❖	❖	❖	❖	❖
Singapore	❖	❖	❖	❖	❖	❖
Thailand	❖	❖	❖	❖	❖	❖
Vietnam	❖	❖	❖	❖	❖	❖
Laos	❖	❖	❖			
Myanmar	❖	❖	❖			
China		❖	❖	❖	❖	❖
Japan		❖	❖	❖	❖	❖
South Korea		❖	❖	❖	❖	❖
Australia		❖	❖	❖	❖	
New Zealand		❖	❖	❖	❖	
US		❖	❖	❖	❖	
Canada		❖	❖	❖	❖	
Russia		❖	❖	❖	❖	
EU		❖	❖			❖[1]
India		❖	❖			
Cambodia	❖					
Mongolia		❖				
Papua New Guinea				❖		
Taiwan				❖	❖	
Hong Kong SAR				❖	❖	
Chile				❖	❖	
Colombia					❖	
Mexico				❖	❖	
Peru				❖	❖	
Pacific Island Nations					❖[2]	

Notes

[1] EU member-states are also represented individually in ASEM

[2] French Pacific Territories have Associate Membership of the PECC

$notes$

Acknowledgments

The author would like to thank Michael Leifer of the London School of Economics and Political Science (LSE) for his comments on an earlier draft of this paper, and Rowena Desouza for her clerical assistance.

Introduction

[1] See, for example, C. Fred Bergsten, 'A Strategic Architecture for the Pacific', in Michael N. Bellows (ed.), *Asia in the Twenty-First Century: Evolving Strategic Priorities* (Washington DC: National Defense University (NDU), 1994), p. 258; Jose T. Almonte, 'Ensuring Security the "ASEAN Way"', *Survival*, vol. 39, no. 4, Winter 1997–98, pp. 80–92; and Yoichi Funabashi, *Asia Pacific Fusion – Japan's Role in APEC* (Tokyo: Chuo Koronsha, 1995).

[2] See, for example, Kent E. Calder, *Pacific Defense – Arms, Energy, and America's Future in Asia* (Tokyo: Nihon Keizai Shimbun, 1996); Barry Buzan and Gerry Segal, 'Rethinking East Asian Security', *Survival*, vol. 36, no. 2, Summer 1994, pp. 3–21; and Samuel P. Huntington, *The Clash of Civilizations and the Remaking of World Order* (New York: Simon & Schuster, 1996).

Chapter 1

[1] Yoshibumi Wakamiya, 'Asianism in Japan's Postwar Politics', in Tadashi Yamamoto and Charles E. Morrison (eds), *Japan and the United States in Asia Pacific: The Challenge for Japan in Asia* (Tokyo: Japan Centre for International Exchange, 1995), p. 16.

[2] See Naoki Tanaka, *Ajia no Jidai* (Tokyo: Toyo Keizai Shinpo-sha, 1996), chapter 2.

[3] 'The Constitution of Japan, Chapter II', www.ntt.co.jp/japan/constitution.

[4] For an overview of Japan's

security dilemma up to the early 1980s, see Yukio Sato, 'The Evolution of Japanese Security Policy', in Robert O'Neill (ed.), *Security in East Asia* (Aldershot, Hants: Gower Publishers for the IISS, 1984), pp. 19–61.

[5] See 'Statement at Williamsburg', www.library.utoronto.ca/www/g7/83secur.htm.

[6] Kazuo Ogura, 'Japan's Asia Policy, Past and Future', *Japan Review of International Affairs*, vol. 10, no. 4, Winter 1996, pp. 1–15. When he wrote this article, Ogura was Japan's Deputy Minister for Foreign Affairs.

[7] See Mike M. Mochizuki, 'Japanese Security Policy', in Michael J. Green and Mike M. Mochizuki, *The US–Japan Security Alliance in the Twenty-First Century* (New York: Council on Foreign Relations (CFR), 1998), pp. 25–52.

[8] Mie Kawashima, 'Hashimoto Calls on Nations "To Build Trust" with Beijing', *Kyodo News*, Tokyo, 14 January 1997, in Foreign Broadcast Information Service (FBIS), *Daily Report*, EAS-97-009, 15 January 1997.

[9] *1991 Diplomatic Blue Book: Japan's Diplomatic Activities* (Tokyo: Ministry of Foreign Affairs (MOFA), 1991), p. 21.

[10] The four principles governing Japan's Overseas Development Assistance (ODA) are: '1) Environmental conservation and development should be pursued in tandem. 2) Any use of ODA for military purposes or for aggravation of international conflicts should be avoided. 3) Full attention should be paid to trends in recipient countries' military expenditures, their development and production of mass destruction weapons and missiles, their export and import of arms, etc., so as to maintain and strengthen international peace and stability, and from the viewpoint that developing countries should place appropriate priorities in the allocation of their resources on their own economic and social development. 4) Full attention should be paid to efforts for promoting democratization and introduction of a market-orientated economy, and the situation regarding the securing of basic human rights and freedoms in the recipient countries.' See *Japan's Official Development Assistance, Annual Report 1996* (Tokyo: MOFA, 1997), p. 211.

[11] 'New National Defense Program Outline', www.jda.go.jp/policy/f_work/jndp/1_2_e.html.

[12] 'Completion of the Review of the Guidelines for US–Japan Defense Cooperation', www.jda.go.jp/policy/f_work/sisin4_.htm.

[13] Hitoshi Tanaka, '"Pacifist Japan" Reconsidered', *Gaiko Forum*, no. 107, July 1997, pp. 35–40. Also see Tanaka, 'An Inside Look at the Defense Guidelines Review', interview with Hisayoshi Ina, *Japan Echo*, vol. 24, no. 5, December 1997, pp. 30–33.

[14] On this debate, see Kenichiro Sasae, *Rethinking Japan–US Relations*, Adelphi Paper 292 (London: Brassey's for the IISS, 1994), p. 55.

[15] Mochizuki, 'Japanese Security Policy'.

[16] 'Statement by Prime Minister Tomiichi Murayama (15 August 1995)', www.mofa.go.jp/announce/press/pm/murayama/9508.html.

[17] 'Japan–Republic of Korea Joint Declaration: A New Japan–Republic of Korea Partnership

towards the Twenty-First Century, October 1998', www.mofa.go.jp.
[18] In this context, see Funabashi, *Asia Pacific Fusion*, especially chapter 13.

Chapter 2

[1] Michael Richardson, 'Beijing Plays Key Role as East Asians Improve Ties', *International Herald Tribune*, 24 November 1997, p. 8.
[2] 'Sino-US Joint Statement October 29, 1997', *Beijing Review*, 17–23 November 1997.
[3] Lee Kim Chew, 'S-E Asia Gets East Asia's Vote of Confidence', *Straits Times*, 17 December 1997, p. 1.
[4] 'Jiang Vows China Will Be Good Neighbor to ASEAN', *International Herald Tribune*, 17 December 1997, p. 4.
[5] See, for example, Caspar Weinberger and Peter Schweizer, *The Next War* (Washington DC: Regnery Publishing, 1997); and Richard Bernstein and Ross H. Munro, *The Coming Conflict with China* (New York: Knopf, 1997).
[6] David Shambaugh, 'Chinese Hegemony over East Asia by 2015?', *Korean Journal of Defense Analysis*, vol. 9, no. 1, Summer 1997, p. 28.
[7] Joseph S. Nye, 'China's Re-emergence and the Future of the Asia-Pacific', *Survival*, vol. 39, no. 4, Winter 1997–98, pp. 65–79. Nye, a strong proponent of engagement, shaped the Clinton administration's China policy as Assistant Secretary of Defense for International Security Affairs in 1994–95. For a variation on the containment theme, see Gerald Segal, 'East Asia and the "Constrainment" of China', *International Security*, vol. 20, no. 4,

Spring 1996, pp. 107–35.
[8] Alastair Iain Johnston, 'China's New "Old Thinking"', *International Security*, vol. 20, no. 3, Winter 1995–96, pp. 5–42; Tomoyuki Kojima, 'China's Present Condition and Future Outlook', *Asia-Pacific Review*, vol. 4, no. 2, Autumn/Winter 1997, p. 106.
[9] Kiyoshi Tanaka, '20 Seiki – Don'na; Idai Datta No Ka', *Yomiuri Shimbun*, 8 February 1998, p. 6.
[10] Denny Roy, 'Hegemon on the Horizon?', *International Security*, vol. 19, no. 1, Summer 1994, pp. 149–68.
[11] Lee Kuan Yew, Keynote Address, IISS Conference, Singapore, September 1997.
[12] Thomas J. Christensen, 'Chinese Realpolitik', *Foreign Affairs*, vol. 75, no. 5, September–October 1996, p. 44. Also see Denny Roy, 'The Foreign Policy of Great-Power China', *Contemporary South-East Asia*, vol. 19, no. 2, September 1997, especially pp. 125–27.
[13] '"Economic Power has the Right to be a Military Power", Says the Chinese Deputy Chief of Staff', *Nihon Keizai Shimbun*, 30 April 1980, p. 2.
[14] Then Chinese Vice-Foreign Minister Tang Jixuan in discussion with Japanese Ambassador to China Yoshiyasu Sato. See 'Sino-Japanese Relations in the Twenty-First Century', *Gaiko Forum*, no. 110, September 1997, p. 32.
[15] 'Security Dialogue Between Japan, US and China Begins', *Asahi Shimbun*, 16 July 1998, p. 2.
[16] Calder, *Pacific Defense.*

Chapter 3

[1] See Almonte, 'Ensuring Security the "ASEAN Way"'; and Jusuf

Wanandi, 'Thinking Strategically about Security in Pacific Asia', in Hanns Maul, Gerald Segal and Jusuf Wanandi (eds), *Europe and the Asia-Pacific* (London: Routledge, 1998), pp. 116–22.

[2] ASEAN's dialogue partners are: Australia; Canada; China; the European Union; India; Japan; South Korea; New Zealand; Papua New Guinea; Russia; and the US.

[3] 'The Bangkok Declaration, Thailand, 8 August 1967', www.asean.or.id. Beyond these three central objectives, ASEAN states also aimed to 'provide assistance to each other in the form of training and research facilities in the educational, professional, technical and administrative spheres'; to 'collaborate more effectively for the greater utilization of their agriculture and industries [and] the expansion of their trade'; to 'promote South-East Asian studies'; and to 'maintain close and beneficial cooperation with existing international and regional organizations with similar aims and purposes'.

[4] In an early example of the way in which this spirit of community has facilitated compromise, Malaysia and the Philippines normalised relations in May 1969 after breaking them off the previous year because of a territorial dispute.

[5] See 'Treaty of Amity and Cooperation in Southeast Asia, Indonesia, 24 February 1976', www.asean.or.id.

[6] Takashi Tajima, 'China and South East Asia: Strategic Interests and Policy Prospects', in O'Neill (ed.), *Security in East Asia*.

[7] See Kishore Mahbubani, 'ASEAN Magic', *Gaiko Forum*, no. 91, April 1996, pp. 50–55.

[8] *Ibid.*, p. 54.

[9] US Department of State, 'Secretary of State Madeleine K. Albright, Statement to the ASEAN Post-Ministerial Conference, Kuala Lumpur, Malaysia, 28 July 1997', www.secretary.state.gov.

[10] N. Takoyama and Y. Hasegawa, 'Naisei Fukansho Meguri Kiretsu', *Yomiuri Shimbun*, 22 September 1998.

Chapter 4

[1] Kishore Mahbubani has suggested that 'Both sides have retreated from the debate with a sense of embarrassment that each side may have overstated its case'. See Mahbubani, *Can Asians Think?* (Singapore: Times Books International, 1998), p. 12.

[2] *Ibid.*

[3] Kishore Mahbubani, 'The Pacific Way', *Foreign Affairs*, vol. 74, no. 1, January–February 1995, p. 103.

[4] Lee Kuan Yew, quoted in Fareed Zakaria, '"Culture is Destiny" – A Conversation with Lee Kuan Yew', *ibid.*, vol. 73, no. 2, March–April 1994, p. 111.

[5] Lynette Clemetson, 'Hard Work, Toil and Tears – Anwar on Asian Values and Western Conspiracies', *Newsweek*, 1 September 1997, pp. 26–27.

[6] Zakaria, '"Culture is Destiny"', p. 111.

[7] Anand Panyarachun, 'Forging a Partnership with the New Asia', *Asia-Pacific Review*, vol. 4, no. 2, Autumn/Winter 1997, pp. 1–6.

[8] Rabindrinath Tagore (1861–1941) was an influential literary and political figure who sought to build a bridge between Western and Eastern thought, arguing that Indian social systems needed to

modernise to ensure the productive political freedom of the individual. Meng-tzu (372–289 BC) was, like Confucius, a political theorist. As a Confucian, he based his system of thought on the concept of *jen* ('humaneness' or 'benevolence'), and from this argued for a form of 'social contract' under which, if a ruler failed to ensure peace and stability, popular revolt was permissible.

[9] For an expression of this view, see Kim Dae Jung, 'Is Culture Destiny?: The Myth of Asia's Anti-Democratic Values', *Foreign Affairs*, vol. 73, no. 6, November–December 1994, pp. 189–94.

[10] Francis Fukuyama, *The End of History and the Last Man* (New York: Free Press, 1992).

[11] Samuel P. Huntington, 'The Clash of Civilizations?', *Foreign Affairs*, vol. 72, no. 3, Summer 1993, p. 22; and Huntington, *The Clash of Civilizations and the Remaking of World Order*.

[12] Kazuo Ogura, 'A Call For a New Concept of Asia', *Japan Echo*, vol. 20, no. 3, Autumn 1993, p. 41.

[13] For this 'Westernistic' version, see Barry Buzan and Gerald Segal, *Anticipating the Future: Twenty Millennia of Human Progress* (London: Simon & Schuster, 1998).

Chapter 5

[1] 'Reforms for the New Era of Japan and ASEAN', policy speech by Prime Minister Ryutaro Hashimoto, Singapore, 14 January 1997.

[2] For a negative view of the prospects for a Pacific community, see Robert A. Manning and Paula Stern, 'The Myth of the Pacific Community', *Foreign Affairs*, vol. 73, no. 6, November–December 1994, pp. 79–93.

[3] Of APEC's original members, six were ASEAN states – Brunei, Indonesia, Malaysia, the Philippines, Singapore and Thailand – and six non-ASEAN states – Australia, Canada, Japan, South Korea, New Zealand and the US.

[4] 'Connecting the APEC Community', APEC Economic Leaders' Declaration, Vancouver, 25 November 1997.

[5] C. Fred Bergsten, 'APEC and World Trade: A Force for Worldwide Liberalisation', *Foreign Affairs*, vol. 73, no. 3, May–June 1994, p. 20.

[6] 'The Transatlantic Front', *The Economist*, 14 March 1998, p. 106.

[7] See Lee, 'S-E Asia Gets East Asia's Vote of Confidence'; and Yukihisa Nakatsu, 'China Takes Steady Steps towards Promoting Multipolarisation', *Yomiuri Shimbun*, 17 December 1997.

[8] Richard Higgot, 'Shared Response to the Market Shocks?', *World Today*, vol. 40, no. 1, January 1998, pp. 4–6.

[9] Michael Leifer, *The ASEAN Regional Forum*, Adelphi Paper 302 (Oxford: Oxford University Press for the IISS, 1996), p. 52.

[10] *Ibid.*, p. 58.

[11] Jusuf Wanandi, 'ASEAN's China Strategy: Towards Deeper Engagement', *Survival*, vol. 38, no. 3, Autumn 1996, p. 121.

[12] Dong-Ik Shin and Gerald Segal, 'Getting Serious About Asia–Europe Security Cooperation', *Survival*, vol. 39, no. 1, Spring 1997, pp. 138–55.

[13] See *The Rationale and Common Agenda for Asia–Europe Cooperation* (London: Council for Asia–Europe Cooperation, 1998), chapter 1.

[14] See, for example, John Naisbitt, *Megatrends Asia* (Tokyo: Hayakawa, 1996). Naisbitt identifies eight trends in Asia that, he argues, are changing the world; the trend from nation-states to (Chinese) networks is the first. Kenichi Ohmae argues that Asia's future lies in the connections between regions within nation-states. See, for example, Kenichi Ohmae and Kazuhisa Oriyama, *Ajia Gasshukoku no Tanjo* (Tokyo: Daiyamondo-sha, 1995). See also Toshio Watanabe, 'The New Shape of East Asian Economic Development: From Dependency to Self-Reliance', *Japan Review of International Affairs*, vol. 11, no. 1, Winter/Spring 1997, p. 40.

Conclusion

[1] Hashimoto, 'Reforms for the New Era of Japan and ASEAN'.